D0452227

*The Sheep's in the Meadow,
Raccoon's in the Corn*

The Sheep's in the Meadow, Raccoon's in the Corn

or, *Life in the Country*

Marguerite Hurrey Wolf

Illustrations by Adelaide Murphy

The New England Press
Shelburne, Vermont

©1979 by The New England Press
ALL RIGHTS RESERVED

The New England Press
P.O. Box 525
Shelburne, Vermont 05482

Library of Congress Catalog Card Number: 79-91349
ISBN: 0-933050-03-8

*For the two latest additions to our family—
our new sister-in-law, Etta Philips, and our
new grandson, Peter Michael Ström.*

The author and publisher are grateful to the following publications for
their permission to use material in this book:
Burlington Free Press, "Seed Catalogues: A Mid-Winter Night's
Dream," March, 1977; *Chittenden,* "Reflections in an Autumn
Pool," October, 1973; "Yes, Virginia, There Is a Spring," April, 1972;
Christian Home, "Heard Any *Good* News Lately?" February, 1971,
Copyright ©1970 by Graded Press; *New England Homestead,* "Do
Ladies Drive Trucks?" January, 1968; "Pumpkins," March, 1968;
Vermont Times-Journal, "Sounds of Spring," March, 1977; "The Un-
common Christmas," December, 1976; *Window of Vermont,*
"February," February, 1978; "Mr. McGregor, Where Are You Now?"
May, 1977.

Printed by Queen City Printers, Burlington, Vermont
PRINTED IN THE UNITED STATES OF AMERICA

Contents

The Case for Country Living: An Introduction
    of Sorts   3

Seed Catalogues—A Mid-Winter Night's Dream   8

Who Needs an Introduction?   13

February   16

The Day My Status Lost Its Quo   19

Yes, Virginia, There Is a Spring   23

Sounds of Spring   26

Mr. McGregor, Where Are You Now?   29

Don't Call the Plumber   33

A Treeful of Hummingbirds   38

Do Ladies Drive Trucks?   43

Hang Your Clothes on the Hickory Limb   48

Our Woodchuck Would   52

Why Can't a Man Be More like a Woman?   56

What Do You Mean, Birdbrain?   63

Try "Open Sesame" on Your Pill Bottle   68

In Praise of Pigs   71

Heard Any *Good* News Lately?   76

Tell Me Not in Mournful Numbers   80

Who's Sheepish Now?   84

Happy the Bride the Rain Falls On   89

Pumpkins   93

Reflections in an Autumn Pool   97

I'm Tired of Keeping a Stiff Upper Lib!   99

What's Good about November?   102

Our Country Night Life   105

Cops and Robbers   108

The Winter of My Content   115

The Uncommon Christmas   121

"No Orchard's the Worse for the Wintriest
     Storm"   125

The Sheep's in the Meadow, Raccoon's in the Corn

The Case for Country Living: An Introduction of Sorts

So you want to live in the country? When was the last time you lifted a hundred-pound grain bag, shovelled out a pig-pen, or split a cord of wood?

When some of our city friends talk wistfully about retiring to the country, planting a garden, keeping a few chickens, boiling sap, and heating with wood, George and I try to avoid each other's eyes.

The facts are that you have to be able-bodied to be self-sufficient in the country. Now I'm not ready to label myself *hors de combat*, but my muscular strength and brittleness of bone are not of the same caliber that they were twenty-seven years ago when we became "year-round summer people" and quite literally went wild not only with hogs but also sheep, turkeys, chickens, a horse, and transient other creatures.

Fortunately we've learned a few skills in our years of ruralization. We no longer have to chase pigs because we're smarter at preventing their escape. We never did plan to have them escape. We were just too inexperienced to provide proper enclosures, and we underestimated the ability of a small pig, ten inches in diameter, to squeeze through a three-inch gap in the fence. I still don't know how they do it. I only know that you can leave two six-week-old pigs snuffling happily in the shavings in their pen, go back to the house to wash the breakfast dishes, look out the window, and see their round little rumps disappearing over a knoll in the pasture. A cow, who exhibits a minimum of cerebral activity on most occasions, can find the only weak spot in the fence and hightail it into your garden before you've groaned "Oh no!" And the damage a foraging cow, or three, can do to a garden is not so much what she eats as what she tramples with her big splayed feet when you chase her out. At those moments I agree with Robert Russell Wicks, Dean of the Chapel at Princeton, who said, "The rear end of a cow has very little to recommend it."

These errant cows were never our own. We never kept cows for one good reason—me. You can't go away for a weekend and expect a neighbor to milk your cows, clean the barn, and wash the pails. When George used to be asked how much we farmed, he invariably replied, "As much as my wife's back can stand." It was flexible enough then to stand a lot, but it stiffened at the mention of a cow.

Sheep, who seem to me to be genetically hollow between the ears, will dedicate themselves to the cause of freedom and follow their slightly brighter leader to greener pastures. One winter our ram found that in one corner of their enclosure the snow and ice had piled up high enough to that he could leap over the fence, and the ewes were right behind him. As the snow melted, it required more and more effort. When the snow was entirely gone he still would go to that spot and make a few valiant efforts to clear the fence. By then that part of the fence was no lower than any other but the ram, being a creature of little brain as well as of habit, still would rush to that corner wondering where his muscle went.

We no longer have a horse because Patty, who at twelve thought that life was meaningless without a horse, now gets all the exercise she can tolerate riding herd on her two small sons in Finland. We plan to have a beef animal and have added a couple of sheep and two geese to our previous modest census of two pigs and twenty laying hens. Of course one pig and five hens would supply two people with all the eggs, poultry, and pork they use. But five hens would be pretty chilly in the barn at twenty below, and we think two pigs are not only warmer but chummier than one. We sell six dozen eggs a week, and we sell half of one pig to a neighbor.

Of course to earn money raising chickens, as some of our friends daydream about, you'd have to go into volume, perhaps a thousand; and that would lead to expensive housing, feed by the ton, manure to be shovelled out, and packaging and distributing of eggs and poultry. This would require hired help, and they don't expect to do the chores for fun and exercise the way you do.

The pig and chicken manure goes on the garden, and the garden is our best source of produce, economy, exercise, and delight in the growth and consumption of forty kinds of vegetables that make the best ones in the supermarket look as though they should be labeled "reduced for quick sale." I know no greater satisfactions than cutting a handful of amethyst-tipped asparagus spears, tasting the first peas and sweet corn, or tossing a salad made of three kinds of leaf lettuce, a scallion, and a couple of radishes.

Our garden, approximately forty by sixty, provides all of our vegetables except the celery and lettuce that I buy in the winter. Unfortunately, we also supply half our corn to raccoons in spite of the electric fence and once or twice have served gourmet meals to uninvited woodchucks.

In your bucolic dream no doubt you plan to heat with

wood. Everyone loves an open fire, but a fireplace warms the heart more than the home and wafts most of its B.T.U.'s up the chimney. But stoves are another matter and think of what you'll save! While you're cerebrating you'd better think of the cold, or warm, facts. You will be doing it for economy so of course you'll cut your wood yourself, saw and split it, stack it, carry it into the house, call upon Vulcan to ignite your sometimes fireproof wood, carry out the ashes, and dismantle and clean the chimney. This country caper heats all right, the woodcutter as well as the house. Tight woodstoves are wonderfully efficient in producing heat. They also produce dust throughout the house, bits of flora and occasional fauna on the rugs, and tarnish on the silver. My mother never told me about that. She never told me because my parents thought they were improving their lot when they switched happily from shovelling coal into a furnace to flicking a lever on the thermostat that activated the oil burner. Of course that was before coal and oil were believed destined to join the other extinct fossils in the Museum of Natural History.

Then why do we do it? Because we like the idea of self-sufficiency and because the escalating costs of other fuels make economy look more attractive than convenience. We haven't reached the level of our pioneer ancestors who bought only salt, tea, coffee, and baking soda, called *salteratus* in the old record books. We're still dependent and addicted to cars for transportation and a grocery bill that inflates faster than our economies are able to deflate it. But think what it would be if we didn't produce our own pork, eggs, chicken, vegetables and some fruits!

And the truth is that economy isn't the real motivating force. We enjoy the welcoming snorts and snuffles of our pigs, the soothing murmuring and muttering of our hens, the miracle of a zucchini seed turning into an enormous lush plant with tropical-looking orange blossoms and a never ending supply of squash from July till frost, the reassuring façade of a stacked woodpile, and the awareness of being in partnership with nature.

We may rail against the marauding raccoons when our corn is barely ripe, but we love to watch them scratch for sunflower seeds under our bird feeders on a winter night. We complain about the drifting snow and the potholes and the boredom of tweezing pinfeathers from a molting chicken, but the sirens of the city are not the ones that enticed Ulysses, or us. With an increasing awareness that we are mortal after all, how else would we want to spend our lives but in conflict and harmony with the five seasons in Vermont?

Seed Catalogues—A Mid-Winter Night's Dream

What is so full of fantasy as a seed catalogue in January? Along with Santa Claus, the Easter Bunny, and Charlie Brown's Great Pumpkin, we cherish the belief that under our tender loving care those tiny seeds will produce scarlet satin tomatoes, glossy purple eggplants, green beans that snap out loud, and pumpkins that require the services of a forklift to get them out of the garden.

This year as the mercury in the thermometer drops down out of sight we muse that there will be no lethal frost after May 15. The soil will be in a fine warm state of tilth. Judicious plantings of marigolds and garlic sets will discourage nematodes and other pests. From the day when you cut the first amethyst-tipped spears of asparagus in May till you dig the last carrot in November, you will be surfeited with succulent garden "sass."

Perhaps that's what keeps gardening people optimistic, a childlike faith that the garden of their dreams is lying dormant under the next forkful of well-rotted manure. And the crazy thing is that every year the gardener's dream does come true, at least in part. If you plant thirty varieties of vegetables, twenty-five of them will do well in any year. Not the same ones each year, of course. In last year's sodden season our lettuce, peas, and spinach looked almost like the ones in the catalogues. But our corn, pumpkins, and winter squash made it obvious that they would have preferred to germinate somewhere in the southwest. Radishes will flourish anyway, but how many radishes can you eat? And we always have so many zucchinis that we could supply the whole neighborhood if the whole neighborhood wasn't trying to unload their zucchinis on us at the same time. If you go to dinner at a gardener's home in July or August, you can be sure you'll be served zucchini thinly disguised as soup, casserole, salad, or bread.

One of the problems is that Mssrs. Burpee, Harris, Ferry, and others grow their seeds and plants in a less erratic climate and in soil that presumably doesn't produce rocks as the main crop the way Vermont gardens do.

I think it is remarkable that we harvest as many delicious, if not always photogenic, vegetables as we do when you consider that it is Russian roulette to plant before Memorial Day and that last year we had a frost on August 30. That squeezed the growing season into three months which isn't enough for some crops. It's not enough for me either, but I quit growing long ago.

We grew prize-winning pumpkins our first year. Beginner's luck? No, stupidity, because I thought pie pumpkins came from *Connecticut Field* seed. But I no longer have the strength to carry fifty-pound pumpkins up from the garden. At the end of a weeding session it is all I can do to resume a vertical stance, pick some vegetables for dinner, and haul the produce and me up the hill.

The testimonials in the seed catalogues make entertaining winter reading. "I had to tell you the fun I've had with *Big*

Girl. I am the talk of the neighborhood." I'll just bet he is! And what about the lady who writes, "My pole beans grew right up onto the roof, and I had to climb a ladder to pick them." Now who has time to play Jack and the Beanstalk when the beans, always a prolific crop, are already chasing you from sink to stove to freezer?

Of course the new burpless cucumber may make you more socially acceptable, and if conversation seems to be wilting, you can flash a handful of purple beans or a bunch of golden beets under your guests' noses. The beans and beets are no tastier than the conventionally colored ones, but they will make your guests refuse another drink, and that's an economy move right there. They also do a double take when the same purple beans reappear on the dinner table looking as green as the standard varieties. Spaghetti squash is another eye widener. Besides it is free of certain faults that spaghetti has like boiling over, sticking to the colander, and making you fat.

The real conversation stopper is the Lady Godiva pumpkin which has—you guessed it—naked edible seeds. In fact, it is grown for its seeds rather than its flesh, which I don't think was the case for Lady Godiva. But if you want an all-purpose pumpkin which does everything that a pumpkin can do but keep your wife, try the new *Triple Threat* which is good for pies, jack-o-lanterns, and also hull-less seeds. What I'd really like is a pumpkin with prickle-less stems! They're not likely to breed out prickles as long as the myth persists that raccoons don't like to bruise their little paws on the pumpkin vines. That's why grandpa always planted his pumpkins in the corn rows. I think that underestimates both grandpa and the raccoons. Yankee thrift probably prompted grandpa to plant them that way to save space. No Vermont raccoon I've ever known has been wary of perforated paws. I've known quite a

few, and their leathery palms are a lot tougher than mine even when mine are calloused by gardening. In a recent issue of *Organic Gardening and Farming* there was a letter suggesting that if you put a *Kentucky Wonder* seed in each hill of corn it will deter raccoons. The fuzz on the underside of the leaves gets on the coon's nose; he doesn't like it and won't go up after the corn!

The truth is that in spite of the annual crop of stones, the short growing season, the black flies that bedevil you in June, and the beasts and bugs who think you planted your garden for their delectation, the daily miracle of growth satisfies some primeval urge to be in productive partnership with the earth and the changing seasons. And working in a garden is therapeutic. Any problem shrinks as you pick your way along a row of beans, soothed by the hum of the bees in the squash blossoms and the redwings creaking in the cattails. A garden doesn't solve your problems, but the wide blue sky overhead and the earth warm to your touch assure you that life goes on in spite of your small crises. And if the beans can hunch up out of dark earth, blossom, and be productive, so can you.

Who Needs an Introduction?

Unaccustomed as I was to public speaking at the time my first book was published, it came as a great surprise to me to be asked to speak to faculty wives or auxiliary groups. I still don't see why publication between hard covers makes all the difference. I had been writing articles for ten years—in fact the same articles that grew into the books. But it never occurred to anyone, including me, that I should be next on the program between the lemon sherbet and the treasurer's report.

Of course program chairmen are notably desperate. I've been one, upside down in the barrel scraping away at the bottom. I suppose the myth is that if the tools of your craft are words they can spill out of your mouth as easily as from your fingertips. In my case they often do because the sort of writing I do springs from reaction rather than research, but there are distinguished authors who can't say a complete sentence out loud and there are polished speakers who write as though they had been assigned a fifth grade composition.

I must admit that my hands dripped and my pulse pounded in my ears the first few times I heard, "And now it is my pleasure to present"—and realized that in the next moment it would be me or an abyss of silence. But pretty soon I began to listen to the introductions because I found out some interesting things about myself. Because it says on the dust jackets of my books that George was a Medical College dean and that I once taught nursery school, I have been introduced as a dean of Nursing, a professor of Nursing, a writer for the Medical College, a nurse at the University hospital, and a "deaner" at the Medical College—the chap who takes care of the experimental animals and the laboratory apparatus. It was lovely to hear once that I had written nearly one hundred books instead of four.

When we were in Kansas, I was often introduced as a writer from Maine or New Hampshire because to many midwesterners all the states in New England are interchangeable. My second book, whose title is *How To Be a Doctor's Wife Without Really Dying,* has been called *How To Be a Doctor's Wife Without Really Trying* which isn't fair. I did! I did! And my name comes out Margaret, Marjorie, or even Virginia rather than Marguerite.

All these things happened because the person who made the introduction had glanced hastily at the dust jacket and was too nervous about her role to check the facts. The really funny moments, as always, are the ones that aren't intended to be funny at all. When we lived in Weston, Massachusetts, a lady phoned and invited me to a cocktail party. When, in some embarrassment, I had to admit that I couldn't remember her, she said, "Oh, we've never met. But the man at the cleaner's told me you were an author, and I've got an artist and a musician for my party but I need an author!"

Another phone call surprised me with, "Are you the lady who talks for free?"

One time in Walter Hard's Johnny Appleseed Book Store

in Manchester, Vermont, a matronly lady overheard Mr. Hard asking me about my books. She catapulted to the door and sang out to her friends waiting in the car, "Girls! Come in, quick. There's a real live author in here!" Mr. Hard and I feigned deafness while they looked me up and down from all angles, commented on the fact, true enough, that I am not as pretty as the picture on the dust jacket, and then wrote down the titles of the books "so we can get them from the library."

I have been introduced as an "old and dear friend" of a lady I had met the week before and as someone "who came to Kansas from Boston but is much nicer than you would expect." A sweet young medical student's wife said in her introduction that it was "hard to believe that anyone as old as Mrs. Wolf could know how we feel."

It is hard enough to find any resemblance between me and the talented speaker described in the flowery introductions that so many older women feel are required, but the most emotional one was at a professional meeting in Missouri. The program chairman said that she had read my first book the night before and had been so "moved by its sheer poetry that—that—sob—" she burst into tears and fled from the room. I yearned to follow her out and into a handy hole in the ground, but there were all those upturned bewildered faces who had been led to believe that my books were funny. It was uphill work eliciting the first chuckle or two, but I thought I was doing pretty well under the circumstances until it was over and the presiding lady said, "and now, before we adjourn I want to thank Mrs. Wolf for not charging us a speaker's fee because now we can get a really *good* speaker next month!"

February

February, in my childhood, meant three school holidays: Lincoln's Birthday, Washington's Birthday, and, best of all, Valentine's Day. Of course on Valentine's Day the school was open, but classwork was virtually suspended. Hours had been spent at home sprawled on the floor concocting valentines out of red paper hearts, cupids, bluebirds, and violets, and then gilding the lilies by framing them with heart-shaped lace paper doilies that were mounted on wobbly little folded hinges. It was quite a trick to paste the hinges onto both the back of the doily and the front of the valentine. They were rococo, cockeyed, and oozing with sentimentality and library paste, but we regarded them with the pride of creative accomplishment.

These treasures were carried to school in brown paper bags and stuffed into the square grocery store saltine box, covered with Dennison's red crepe paper, that stood on the teacher's desk.

St. Valentine, a Roman priest, had nothing to do with our lacy creations. That was just an accident of the season that made his day coincide with the celebration of the beginning of the birds' mating season. But long before that the Romans did have their February holiday, the Feast of Terminalia. This fell on February 23 and 24 and was an elaborate ceremony of purification and the setting of boundary stones, which the Romans felt compelled to celebrate or suffer the wrath of the gods.

I am well aware that "good fences make good neighbors," and many Vermont towns still elect fence viewers as hopefully disinterested arbiters of boundaries. We don't worry too much about appeasing Jupiter, the god of boundaries, anymore, and we've shoved Lincoln's and Washington's birthdays together on the nearest Monday. We're not aware of celebrating the Feast of Terminalia, but towards the end of February we celebrate the end of winter by hailing the first signs of spring. Chicadees by then have added "spring soon" to their repertoire. On a warm day the pine needles no longer hang down in stiff clusters but have resumed their flexible erect posture. A flock of redpolls swoops down beneath the bird feeders and swirls up again as though blown by a gust of wind. Our most colorful winter birds come in February. Purple finches and evening grosbeaks make a sudden appearance although in some years the evening grosbeaks arrive in December.

Indoors, signs of spring sprout all over the living room. Our forced tulips and hyacinths are in bloom, seed catalogues spill off the coffee table, and the first pussy willows are stuck in the old pewter coffee pot. We have one pussy willow that has squirrel-soft catkins by Valentine's Day, while the other pussy willows in the neighborhood don't fur out until March.

In mid-February we see a neighbor hanging out his sap buckets. With the thermometer dropping to zero at night and only nudging thirty for a few minutes around noon, he doesn't expect a real run, but his inner calendar is probably goading him into a spring activity. The red squirrels feel it, too, and explore damp spots on the old maples in hopes of discovering the sweet taste of sap.

Lambs used to be born in March in these parts, but now ewes are bred to lamb much earlier. It may benefit man, but I feel sorry for the lambs who are dropped on cold barn floors in January.

Our first robin won't be seen until the end of March. Even then the fields are not always bare, and most of the ground is still frozen. But the wishful thinking towards spring comes in February. The stirring is there. The full Snow Moon seems to have more wattage than other winter full moons. You can read the time on your watch by moonlight, but it is more exciting to walk in the mysterious blue light and to see the familiar landscape camouflaged with surreal shadows.

It is still and cold outside, but the stirring is there. The buds on the maples blur the stark silhouettes, a snowshoe hare bounds into the dark shadows under the pines, and deer walk gingerly on the lacy ice at the edge of the brook testing its strength before stretching down their slender necks to drink from the onyx pool.

There is more snow and all the blustery bravado of March ahead, but the steel grip of winter has been loosened. The tumult of March is a bluff without the hostility of the deep sub-zero cold of January.

The Day My Status Lost Its Quo

What do you do when suddenly your children write "mother's occupation—author" instead of "housewife" and your husband tells you he was introduced not as the Dean of the Medical College but as the husband of the author of *How To Be a Doctor's Wife Without Really Dying*?

You love it, that's what! My family was not particularly impressed after the first time an article of mine was published. They weren't even curious about how it looked. They showed far more enthusiasm for the numbers in print on a check than for my immortal words in print on a page. My husband looked on my literary efforts as a nice harmless hobby that didn't take me out of the house from nine to five, and my children viewed it with the same slight embarrassment caused by other peculiar habits mothers have such as expecting clothes to be picked up, turning down radios, or speaking up at P.T.A. meetings where your own young much prefer you to be seen and not heard.

But as soon as these same stories and some new ones were dignified by a copyright and a Library of Congress number, my status lost its quo.

The first surprise after twenty-five years of apparently anonymous writing was a shower of fan mail. People whose ages ranged from thirteen to ninety-three and who came from such places as Formosa and the Northeast Kingdom wrote to say that I must have had them in mind because the book reminded them of_____, and then they poured out pages of their own experiences with country living or animals or old houses.

One man in Connecticut thought that because we had raised pigs I could tell him how to make sausage that would taste like the kind his grandfather used to make! This puzzled me until I told the story to Wayne Nealy, an old friend in Vermont, who had suffered a stroke and was bedridden. Wayne lay there with his eyes closed, looking so frail that I wondered if he had heard me or had the strength to reply. But after a moment's pause he snorted and said, "That's easy. Tell him to send you the pig his grandfather made the sausage out of."

A research mathematician wrote to say that he not only had lived in Vermont, but had also written a book which he enclosed—*Mathematics and Computers.* I had to thank him immediately for his kindness in sending me the book because I didn't dare reveal that my understanding of mathematics is so limited that I had to be tutored in high school algebra in order to pass a college board exam in the loathsome subject.

A biology professor wrote that because we had discovered treasure in our attic, I might be interested in the enclosed reprints of his work in attics and in the caves of Kentucky—on bats!

I began to be asked to speak at meetings of the ladies' auxiliary, various women's clubs, and Vermont writers, and after each talk people would come up and tell me about their Vermont heritage or their summers on grandfather's farm or where you can find the best blackberries. No one wanted anything except the chance to relive an experience with someone who might understand.

Of course George, my husband, didn't hear these talks, thank goodness. The summer after *Anything Can Happen in Vermont* was published we stopped at a lumberyard to pick up a few things he needed. As always the few things grew into a sizeable order, and George asked the man if he would take a check. The man looked at the check, from a Boston bank, turned it over and said, "Well, I don't know. You're from out of state. I don't know you." And then his eyes lit on the two names in the upper left hand corner, George A. Wolf, Jr. and Marguerite H. Wolf. "Say, your wife the lady who wrote the book? Sure, I'll take your check!"

But in the natural balance of pride and prejudice, the ego of the housewife or the author gets shrunken as well as inflated. One day I went to speak to the Vermont literature course at a local high school. I was sitting in the library with the teacher waiting for the class to begin when the public address system blared out, "Next period Mrs. Wolf will talk to the Vermont literature class in the library." From the other side of the bookshelves a weary teen-age voice moaned, "Who cares?"

Shortly after my first book came out a neighbor phoned to tell me that she had a great idea. She was on the committee for a book fair at her son's school. So she had ordered thirty copies of my book and wondered if I would come that Saturday and sit there and autograph the books as they were sold?

I was flattered but terrified. I knew the purpose of the book fair was to raise money, but who would have heard of my book or want my autograph? I told George that I would probably have to buy back all of my books to which he replied, "Don't you dare!"

So off I went with my pen clutched in my sweaty palm.

When I came home George met me with an expression that showed concern for his pocketbook as well as my psyche.

"How'd it go?"

"Nothing to it. They all sold in the first half hour and they took orders for fifteen more."

"Oh, come on now," he remonstrated. "What really happened?"

"Well, the lady in charge set up a card table and she took off all the dust jackets to show the books' attractive handbound fabric covers, each a different fabric. This was such a novel idea to the grandmas and aunties who were Christmas shopping that they began to haggle over their favorite covers. And one dowager from Beacon Hill bore down on me like a full-rigged schooner, looked me straight in the eye, and said, 'My dear, I don't care *what's* in this book. I *must* have that early American cover for the bedside table in my guest room!' "

Yes, Virginia, There Is
a Spring

When the crows come out of the woods and the farmers go into them to gather the sap from their buckets, I'm glad that I was born too late for those twin rituals, spring cleaning and spring tonic. I can remember what a carpet beater looks like and my mother used to reminisce about the merits of bitters and tonics, but I was never subjected to these ordeals. It was as though the first thrust of a crocus and the drip of the icicles at the eaves evoked in her a tribal memory rather than a current need. Of course I have read about sulphur and molasses—which sounds almost as bad as the oils of the castor bean or the cod's liver which were used in their natural and malodorous state to mortify the flesh in my youth, but I've never smelled or tasted sulphur and molasses, and I'm glad of it.

There was, however, a spring rite our children used to observe when they were growing up in South Burlington. We had a standing offer of an ice cream cone for the child who spotted the first robin. Of course whoever else was along when we went for the ice cream cone got one too, but the glory went to the sharp-eyed one.

They also had a heated contest to see who could collect the most signs of spring. And now that we have wintered over in Vermont for a number of years, I have found that when the chicadees start to say "spring soon" and a raccoon ambles up to sniff the suet put out for the birds, I am looking each day for the new-old portents they ferreted out spring-feverishly. As I recall the rules, advertisements for new clothes or car tune-ups didn't count. Neither did purple plush rabbits or chocolate Easter eggs. But any natural metamorphosis, even if barely perceptible, did. First, of course, is the lengthening of days which became apparent as early as January even though the coldest weather was yet to come. But the additional light at both ends of the day gave us courage to face it. You could get another credit for the first thaw with dripping icicles and granulating snowdrifts. When the fishing shacks disappeared from the lake and a band of open water spread like a dark shadow, the maple trunks blossomed out with pails and spigots and a first crocus exploded into color on the south side of the house.

From then on spring gathers momentum, slowly in our part of the country but noticeably to the eager observer even before the snow fences are rolled up on the side of the highway. No one but a Vermonter would call it spring but to the winter-weary the first dusting of pollen on the pussy willows, the scent of wild onions near the river named after them, and the sharp green of skunk cabbage quicken the heart more than the abundant greens of summer.

The earth steams in the sun and invites the first robins and male red-wings to rest from their territorial contests and come to dinner. Weeping willows glow golden long before they leaf out, and the new growth of the apple twigs shines deep red.

I used to lament the late spring in Vermont, but now I

savor it slowly because, as with many things in life, the anticipation is a large part of the pleasure. There are days when you can see four or five deer grazing between Bolton and Montpelier with no concern for the traffic along the interstate highway. When May finally brings lush green fields crowded with dandelions, apple trees in full blossom, and a spill of lilacs at the corner of every farmhouse, I will have lost count as trillium, wild strawberry, rosy stalks of rhubarb, twin lambs in a meadow, and a wobbly colt are added to my collection.

When Wayne and Ralph Nealy used to let the cows out of their barn in Jericho Center and drive them the two miles to our pasture for the summer, the children and I would go up to watch. Their antics as they sensed the freedom and space after the long winter's confinement were predictable yet wonderfully entertaining. You can't really say that a cow gambols, but they tried, and their ungainly efforts at lighthearted cavorting reduced us to helpless laughter.

Who needs sulphur and molasses, dandelion greens, or sassafras tea? Spring itself is the tonic, and nowhere does it restore the zest for living more than right here and now in Vermont.

Sounds of Spring

I can't see that March has much to do with either lions or lambs. Our neighbors' lambs seem to be dropped earlier and earlier, some even at the end of January, poor things. It can't be much fun to be a newborn lamb on a cold barn floor when the thermometer is hovering on both sides of zero. And of course, our fabled catamount, the nearest thing to a lion in Vermont, was last seen at the end of the nineteenth century.

However the wind does roar, funneling down the valleys and moaning through the pine forests. The brooks roar, too, as they struggle free from the great blocks of ice that pile up on their banks.

But it is the small sounds that tell us it is March even if we are without calendar and blindfolded. The chicadees sing "spring soon" and other almost tuneful phrases. There is the "plink, plink" of maple sap dripping into the buckets. There is the slowed down squish of tires ploughing heavily through the slush and mud on the back roads. The high-pitched squeak of your boots on snow in below zero weather has changed to a slurp as you pull your feet free from the possessive mud.

The first redwings, looking as though they wished they had stayed south with the females and young males for another ten days, creak out their "kankaree" announcing their territorial claims and fighting off intruders with epaulets flashing.

But if you remove the blindfold and look up in the elms and the maples, you discover that every twig is beaded with swelling buds. The willows are beginning to shine golden, and the red osiers are deep crimson. When the snow shrinks back on the south side of the house, there are a dozen snowdrops in full bloom, some of them sticking right up through the last crystallized snow. One of the most modest flowers, their hardiness lifts the spirits of winter-weary Vermonters more than a spray of orchids.

All of the sugar maples blossom out with buckets and plastic bags, and curls of steam drift up out of the sugar houses. The first run is the palest and sweetest, the best of the crop. We tap two old maples and boil down a small amount for our own use. It doesn't seem like a small amount when you are lugging in a heavy pail with two gallons of sap, but those thirty-two cups will boil down to only one cup of syrup.

The flicker, a self-appointed alarm clock, makes sleep impossible when he chooses your metal chimney or roof as the instrument on which to drum his courting message. If you disturb him he flies off protesting loudly "wicker, wicker, wicker"—which sounds suspiciously like "stinker, stinker, stinker!"

You can't hear the change in the light, but you can hear the change that the new welcome warmth is bringing about. The curtain of icicles at the windows drips in contrapuntal rhythm on the deck. A great avalanche of snow loosens and plunges off the roof with an abrasive scrunch followed by a dull thud.

The grumbling of the oil burner or the ping of the electric heating units that were almost continuous in January are now blessedly intermittent.

It is too early for the peepers, the true voice of spring, but in the swamps and along the brooks the melting ice and snow are making a tumultuous departure, freeing the moist earth where the peepers have been hibernating all winter. We can't hear their voices yet, but we know they are stirring and, in response to the new light and warmth, will soon emerge looking for food and a mate.

Was that a robin peeking hopefully at a bare patch on the lawn? Probably not, but if not today then maybe tomorrow. We know there will be more snow and rain and scouring wind and at least a month of mud, but who cares when the fanfare of March sounds announces the imminence of spring?

Mr. McGregor, Where Are You Now?

How long has it been since you've played *Uncle Wiggly?* Remember Nurse Jane Fuzzy-Wuzzy, his muskrat lady housekeeper, the bad Pipsisewah lurking in his den, and the Skillery-Skallery alligator?

One year our whole gardening season was like a continuous game of *Uncle Wiggly*. We made several forward moves with everything growing, the striped cucumber beetles in abeyance and George's rototiller churning up the earth between the rows into a fine state of tilth, only to discover one morning that we had been moved back five to twenty hops by Beatrix Potter's famous rabbit family. Now there is nothing cuter than a baby rabbit, all eyes and twinkly nose, but with all the clover in northern Vermont—it's our state flower for Pete's sake—why did they nip the flowers off our peas, shear the beet leaves as soon as they were three inches high, lop off the lettuce, and prune the parsley?

I always thought Mr. McGregor was a villain, especially when our four-year-old Patty was Flopsy in a school play. She was fascinated by the long white ears of her headdress and by the reaction of her two-year-old sister Debbie, who jumped up and down on her seat in the audience piping shrilly, "Look at Patty with the long ears up!"

At that time Patty's experience with accidents around our house had been largely in terms of Debbie's cavalier attitude towards toilet training so she transposed her lines and announced, "My father made an accident in Mr. McGregor's garden so Mrs. McGregor was sick of cleaning up after him and put him in a pie."

But now I'm on Mr. McGregor's side. What the rabbits, deer, woodchucks, and raccoons did to our garden was no accident. Hasenpfeffer on the menu and no tears.

Each morning, hoe in hand, I approached the garden with a sense of impending doom. What is so rare as a day in June when you find that there has been no overnight damage to the garden? If the latest crop of beans had hunched up out of the ground, the earlier crop sheared off by our vandals had put out new leaves, and the peas were mercifully unscathed and in blossom, it was a moment to savor. I didn't allow my mind to dwell on the fact that those lovely rows of knee-high corn might just as well have been labeled "For raccoons only." In the early years before we fenced the garden, the rate of our corn consumption to theirs was ten ears for the raccoons to every one for the Wolfs. George haunted the garden by moonlight with a gun, heard them chattering happily, shot at several and missed them all. He's a good shot, but a raccoon in a corn patch is an artful dodger.

After hearing my laments about the young broccoli and cabbage plants being eaten down to the stalks, George took his rifle and went down to the garden looking for a woodchuck. I was in the living room and glanced out of the window into the upturned masked face of the biggest raccoon I have ever seen. We stared at each other stupidly for several minutes. It was obvious that she was as myopic as I because she stood on her hind legs and leaned forward to get a better look at me. I was already on my hind legs so I set them in motion and streaked down to the garden to alert George that, like the bluebird of happiness, the quarry was to be found in or near our own kitchen. He reluctantly abandoned tracking the woodchuck and followed me back to the house. As we came in the front door we could hear scratching noises on the outside of the living room wall. George slipped out and sneaked around the end of the house. I froze with my fingers in my ears as is my wont around firearms. Even through my fingers I could hear a shot and then another one and then a wail from George. He had surprised the raccoon climbing halfway up the side of the house. It dropped to the ground. George shot it but the wounded raccoon started around the back of the house. George shot it again and the raccoon somersaulted into the air, landed on the edge of our old well, and fell in! It was a very shallow well—easy enough to fish out a dead raccoon, a little harder to use the water with any degree of enthusiasm.

I put the dead raccoon down in the garden as a threat to other nocturnal foragers but by noon of the next day it seemed advisable to bury it right there—six or seven pounds of fertilizer added to the corn patch which will probably be plundered by six or seven corn-stuffed raccoons in August.

With but one exception, we had established a very organic, productive cycle. Guess who was being left out? We were feeding the black flies, mosquitoes, wild life, and vegetables; in fact, we were feeding everybody but the Wolfs.

I don't want Uncle Wiggly's sassafras candy or baked potato lollypops. I just want our own peas, beans, and corn. But so does every furry creature in Chittenden County. If I'm going to join the natural cycle, it is obvious that I'm not going to get anywhere as a herbivore. The only thing for us to do is to raise the vegetables for the animals and the animals for the people. I understand Euell Gibbons has recipes for opossum and woodchuck in his book *Stalking the Wild Asparagus*. If you know anyone who has a good recipe for roast raccoon, I'll swap a coonskin for it.

Don't Call the Plumber

When we bought the farm in Jericho thirty years ago, its plumbing facilities consisted of a creaky hand pump above the well in the back hall and an outhouse adjoining the wood-shed on the indoor route to the barn. Most farmhouses built in the 1820s were similarly equipped, and our great-grandmothers counted among their blessings the fact that they could make the necessary journeys without braving the elements. Of course they had to brave sub-zero temperatures, but a dry floor was a big improvement over slogging through snow from November through March, and mud until May. Fresh from the towers of Gotham we had grown accustomed to faucets and flush-toilets so that indoor plumbing ranked high on our list of do-it-yourself improvements. Do-it-himself would be more accurate because my knowledge of plumbing is entirely preventive. I just try not to stop up drains and toilets. My skill in re-seating the rubber thing in the back of the toilet to keep it from running the well dry was developed only after we lived in the country.

George convinced himself and me that he must be as bright as the average plumber and that with the help of some government pamphlets he could figure out what he needed, order all the supplies in advance, and put in the plumbing over the Memorial Day weekend. He and I had come up from New York two weekends earlier to plant the garden and dig the hole for the septic tank. So all he had to do in two days was install an electric pump, toilet, sink, and washbasin and string them all up like beads on a chain of copper pipes. Our proposed kitchen had been a bedroom and the bathroom-to-be was what is known in New England as a clothes press, so they were innocent of any pipes or even holes in the walls. We had appropriated a bathroom basin from my parents' attic, but the kitchen sink, the toilet, and all the faucets, drain pipes, T's, unions, plugs, caps, washers, lead pipe, soil pipe, traps, threaders, pipe cutter, wrenches, blowtorch, solder, soldering paste, and other items too numerous to mention were to be delivered the day he arrived.

George and five-year-old Patty drove up on Thursday. Two-year-old Debbie and I came the next day with Ken Schmidt, George's dentist friend, who was to be the plumber's helper. Neither he nor George had plumbed before. It wasn't a required course in either Cornell Medical College or Harvard Dental School. But they were friends from undergraduate days, and Schmitty supplied precision and perfection to match George's raw courage in undertaking the job.

I'm glad I wasn't there the evening George and Patty welcomed the truck from Lanou's plumbing company in Burlington. Its contents were unloaded all over the front lawn so that George could check them off his list: Gargantuan black septic tank, modest white toilet, sink, miles of gleaming copper pipe, and brown bags and boxes of vital accessories. George was so absorbed in this plumber's paradise that he forgot about Patty until she came catapulting down the driveway shouting, "Look out for the cow, Daddy," and skittered past him into the shelter of the house. Sure enough, a large fawn-colored bovine was trotting along behind her, and George was about to comment to the truck driver that one of the reasons we were coming to the country was to acquaint our children with rural flora and fauna when the truck driver leapt smartly up into the back of the truck, pointed at the creature in alarm, and said, "Jeesum crowbars, mister, you gotta be *careful* around them Jersey bulls." Bull? George and what now had suddenly enlarged into a very belligerent bull regarded each other solemnly over the upended toilet in mutual astonishment for a long moment, then the bull, apparently more unnerved by the hardware than by George's immobility, sighed deeply and trotted off down the road.

By the time Schmitty, Debbie, and I arrived, George was so eager to get started that Debbie and I were largely ignored and Schmitty was whisked off to change into jeans and a plumbing frame of mind.

For two days George and Schmitty pored over pencilled diagrams, lit and extinguished blowtorches, cut pipes, and ate in a bemused fashion, a wrench in one hand and a sandwich in the other, while Patty watched hopefully to see if they would put ketchup on a pipe cutter.

When George shouted "hot lead!" we scattered like leaves as he dashed through the room with a little cauldron of bubbling lead to where Schmitty was joining two pipes under the sink. They were deaf to invitations to go swimming and dumb in any language except plumbese.

Finally on Memorial Day morning they pronounced the job done. We stood in awe as the pump was flicked on, the tank filled with pleasant gurglings and splashings, and the toilet was flushed with a flourish. George and Schmitty hugged each other in a demented victory dance and toasted their skill.

"Look, water!" they babbled, turning on first the kitchen and then the bathroom faucets with the wild abandon of men who had crawled for days across the desert.

Then it was time for them to start on the long ride back to New York. They changed into their city clothes, and the little girls and I stood on the denuded front lawn waving them off. For the first time I was to stay in the country to face the bulls and the bats, the thunderstorms and the porcupines, all by myself. I was supposed to be grateful for the plumbing. After all, as George has pointed out for thirty years, what other woman has a sink installed at just the height she chose herself?

It all worked beautifully for several weeks. Then Patty, playing on the side lawn, called out, "Mommy, there's a little fountain out here."

I had just flushed the toilet. I tried it again and peered out the window. Up shot another geyser! I was learning to be a gardener, a paper hanger, and a reluctant cowherd, but the principles of plumbing have never come easily to me. I phoned George.

I reached him at his office at the corner of 68th Street and Madison Avenue. I wonder what the patient sitting across that beautiful desk thought when George said, "Don't use the toilet—go outdoors. And whatever you do, don't call a plumber."

George fixed the geyser the next weekend. It involved taking up the lid of the septic tank and sawing off the pipe that stuck out too far into it. He doesn't recommend that job for a hot July afternoon, but we didn't call a plumber. In fact, in thirty years we never did until this past summer, when in the interest of speed, not lack of plumbing skill, George had to have a new water tank installed. What's more we have had less trouble with the plumbing in that house than in any other house we've ever lived in. Never underestimate the plumbing prowess of a doctor and a dentist. I wonder if a plumber could suggest something besides "Take an aspirin" if I consulted him about a throbbing tooth or an escalating temperature?

A Treeful of Hummingbirds

"The hummingbird is one of the wonders of the countrey, being no bigger than a Hornet, yet hath all the dimensions of a bird . . . For colour she is as glorious as the Rainebow; as she flies, she makes a little humming noise like a Humblebee: Wherefore she is called the Humbird."

—William Wood, *New England Prospect*, 1634

It's not surprising that the tiny hummingbird, unknown in Europe, then and now, amazed William Wood, an early New England colonist. But no one can watch a hummingbird without a sense of wonder. How can it fly backwards—the only bird to do so, hover in the air—a jewel suspended between two wisps of gauze, and then dart forward—flying at speeds of up to thirty miles an hour?

One hummingbird is a small wonder. But a tree full of hummingbirds? By what good fortune was Mrs. Thurston's willow tree in Roxbury, Vermont, singled out as the spot for this phenomenon? Several ornithologists whom I consulted said that the only other hummingbird tree they had heard of was at Holderness, New Hampshire, in the early part of this century.

Mrs. Thurston hung out a hummingbird feeder filled with red-colored sugar water eight years ago and attracted two hummingbirds. The next year there were four. In the summer of 1974 on the day when I first saw them, we estimated that the tree was buzzing, humming, and squeaking with fifty jewelled helicopters, though they are impossible to count because they are in constant motion. Of course there are more feeders now, over a dozen, and they have to be refilled twice a day. It takes six cups of sugar boiled with water to make a gallon of their preferred brew. Left to their own devices the hummingbirds feed on the nectar of such flowers as bee balm, jewelweed, and trumpet flower. They plunge their long, needle-like bills into the blossoms and extend their slender tongues to suck up the sweet juices and also any insects, which form a large part of their diet.

It isn't "she," however, who is as glorious as a "Rainebow." The female has some of the irridescent green coloring on her head and back but only the male has the ruby, glistening throat. Surprisingly this brilliant color looks black in some lights and orange in others because the color is structural like the flashes from a diamond or the blue of the sky and not pigmentary like a red flag. Unless the light falls directly on the bird from behind the observer, very little color can be seen.

Mrs. Thurston's hummingbirds arrive in May. This year they arrived on Mother's Day, which was rather appropriate seeing that Mrs. Thurston is the grandmother of twenty. The males arrive first, a few at a time, and the females a week or two later. Mrs. Thurston is not sure whether or not they nest in the willow tree where they feed. The hummingbird normally builds a tiny thimble-sized nest of plant down plastered

on the outside with bits of lichen. It is placed on top of a branch ten to thirty feet above the ground and resembles a knot on the tree so much that the nests are rarely seen. In this fairy cup the female lays two white pea-size eggs, which hatch out in twelve to sixteen days into bee-size baby hummers. They are fed by the female who plunges her long bill deep into the baby bird's shorter one and regurgitates the food she has gathered. Why she doesn't impale the fledgling on her rapier-like bill is a miracle, but so far there is no record of hummingbird shish kebabs.

In these days of energy shortages, the hummingbird's power plant is an inspiration. Crawford Greenewalt, a noted executive and engineer who has studied and photographed hummingbirds in South and Central America as well as the United States, says that a man with the same energy output would be expending forty horsepower and that he would have to consume 285 pounds of hamburger or 370 pounds of boiled potatoes a day to do it. Hummingbirds prefer sugar supplemented by insects and spiders. Just before they migrate the hummingbirds add fifty percent to their normal weight, all of it fat, for the 2,000 mile trip which includes a 500 mile non-stop flight across the Gulf of Mexico. In order to conserve energy at night they can go into a torpid state with a drop in body temperature and energy output that is one twentieth of that in normal sleep. If their food supply is short, they "nocturnate"—if there is such a word—a form of brief hibernation.

Their wings beat five hundred times a minute which accounts for the fact that thirty percent of their weight is in the wing muscles. To keep themselves in action these little dynamos must refuel every ten to fifteen minutes. Mrs. Thurston is well aware of their needs, and she cheerfully refills each feeder twice a day.

There appear to be many more females than males in the tree, but that is because the young males up until their first molt resemble their mamas.

Sitting under their favored willow tree is a little like being at a busy Lilliputian airport. The air vibrates with tiny dive bombers and helicopters. Fortunately they seem to have no fear of or grudge against humans and are not disturbed by an audience. But they are fiercely pugnacious among themselves and will attack and drive off a hawk who could snap them up for hors d'oeuvres if he could figure out how to avoid their threatening skewers.

Mrs. Thurston is very gracious about sharing her aviary phenomenon with anyone who is interested in the birds. She asks only that you sign her visitors' book. Many of her visitors bring sugar. With the soaring cost of food, her sugar bill amounts to about five dollars a week. This summer her guests have kept her well supplied with sugar.

A small token of sugar can in no way be equated with the unique experience of sitting at the edge of the swaying curtain of weeping willow leaves enveloped in a susurration of tiny jewelled hummingbirds.

Do Ladies Drive Trucks?

"My face, I don't mind it
Because I'm behind it
The people in front get the jar."

This was brought home to me a week after a red, half-ton Ford pickup truck became our second car. Of course I had been initiated gradually. When a second car became a necessity in our family, I had been entranced with the Army Jeep we bought, even though children had a tendency to fall out the back, and icy winds had more than a tendency to whistle in around the canvas and isinglass and nudge me in the front seat. We needed something useful and rugged to fit my role as a country wife. My husband, as Dean of the Medical College at the University of Vermont, could only farm as much as his wife's back could stand. The Jeep had limitations in space and comfort, so after remarking kiddingly to each other, "What we need is a half-ton truck," we finally realized that a truck *was* what we needed.

George drove it home victoriously one afternoon, and the next day I steered it happily along the main street of Burlington and parked in front of Preston's jewelry store with as much pride as though it had been a Mercedes Benz. As I was about to leap to the ground, a small boy tugged at his mother's coat and gasped, "Look, Mommy, a lady in a red truck! Ladies don't drive trucks."

He wasn't criticizing my character. He was stating a fact based on observation. He would have been equally surprised to see a lady on a fire engine. For that matter, so would I. Of course I never saw myself driving the truck. I thought George looked pretty funny, driving it in a black Homburg, a relic of his Madison Avenue practice days. And Patty looked as though the truck were driving her, when she perched behind the wheel. I was so happy inside the truck that I never gave my image a thought. It was the handiest conveyance that ever shared our garage with a "soft car." You had a panoramic view high in the cab surrounded by wide windows and no chrome gadgets. It held twelve Brownie Scouts with the sound of their songs and squeals mercifully streaming out in our wake. Several bicycles could be slid easily into the back as well as any number of skis, grain bags, ten-foot planks, and even our horse whose name, inappropriately perhaps, was Lady. Without the truck we couldn't have moved our menagerie of pigs, sheep, kittens, turkeys, children, and other assorted lares and penates from South Burlington to Jericho and back each summer. We would have had to change our habits, and habits are harder to change than conveyances. It was useful to our friends as well. Ethan Sims used it to move old beams that had been part of the spire of the Unitarian church. John Teal borrowed it to transport a horse either to or from his farm on Camel's Hump, and he was used to transporting musk ox calves by plane from the arctic tundra to the sub-arctic climate of Huntington.

It was a wonderfully versatile vehicle, with none of the

shortcomings of a "soft car." Melted popsicles, shavings, and pig manure could be washed out in a few minutes leaving nothing clinging, either literally or by a not too subtle hint of fragrance. When we went *en famille* to Maine in the "soft car," Debbie's starfish that she had carefully collected from the tide pools left a fishy aroma in the trunk that we had to live with until we turned in the car. A scratch or dent on the car was a major catastrophe, but the nicks and gouges on the truck were only battle scars that enhanced its character. The chassis was so high off the ground that we could hurtle up lumber roads or across the fields without being hung up on a boulder or damaging all those useful things like exhaust pipes and axles which they tuck underneath. The mechanism under the hood seemed simpler and much more accessible to me. If it didn't start on a dewy morning, I could identify the spark plugs, wipe them off with Kleenex, and be on my way. If it conked out after a long haul over dusty and sandy roads, Patty taught me that a sharp tap with a hammer on that big round thing in the engine loosened the grain of sand and off we roared again. There was no trunk to lock your keys into by mistake and no cloth upholstery to capture and preserve the prints of little feet.

Of course it was a bit trying for our teen-age daughters to be picked up in front of the high school by a mother in a red truck. But when you are thirteen and fifteen anything your mother does is unbearable. They would scrunch down as far out of sight as possible and plead with me to make a fast get-away. But the truck gave them a certain rapport with the high school boys who were thumbing rides up Main Street, and often we had collected three or four healthy specimens before we had climbed the hill to the U.V.M. campus. Given the choice, the boys would have preferred a sports car or any car without a muffler which would have called attention to themselves, but when the choice was between Shank's mare or riding in the back of the truck, where they could war-whoop or whistle at passers-by, depending on the sex, they leapt over the sides, spraying books, track shoes, and large feet with no damage to the truck. I can think of a dozen young men now in Cambridge, Oklahoma, the Virgin Islands, or the Navy with whom I had frequent, limited, and identical conversations, "Thanksfertheride" and " 'Sokay."

As a matter of fact our truck wasn't really conducive to conversation. The driver couldn't hear what the boys in back said, thank goodness; and it was probably just as well that they couldn't hear an occasional blasphemy from the front seat.

In fact one time the truck was a real conversation stopper. We had been invited to drive up to Greensboro, a distance of sixty-five miles, for luncheon with old New York friends, Beth and Roudy Roudebush. It was an annual pilgrimage which we enjoyed. A few days before this I had been overambitious in loading crates of chickens into the truck and the muscles of my back wouldn't let me forget it. Driving a car was the most painful position. Sitting in it was almost as bad. In fact the only pain-free position was flat on my back. So George inflated a rubber mattress, put it in the back of the truck, and gave me a pillow and a blanket and we set off for our rendezvous in total, if isolated, comfort.

To shield my eyes from the sun I pulled the blanket over my head. I could see through the blanket but no one could see my face, a very entertaining arrangement. I watched the clouds (pigeon-blue underneath, white cotton candy on top), jet planes preceding their sound by half a sky, an oriole slipping down into her pouch nest slung from a high branch of an elm, bright-blue, top-halves of silos, and square, rosy brick chimneys. George came to a stop in a village, and I found myself directly under a large maple that harbored two unusual birds. They were telephone repairmen, booted and spurred, and presumably cutting some branches that interfered with the wires. At least they were until our truck pulled up underneath them. One man stared at my inert form, decently covered except for a protruding pair of shoes, and nudged his helper who exclaimed, "My gosh! It's a body! Just layin' there, no coffin."

"What you think he's up to? Taking it across the border?"

That was too much for me. As George started up again, I slowly raised my hand, in my best imitation of a corpse, and waved what I hoped looked like a sad farewell to this life.

I've always been sorry George didn't see their faces. Far from showing relief, they were open-mouthed, pop-eyed, and stricken dumb.

It was a moment to savor, and it never could have happened without our old red truck.

Hang Your Clothes
on the Hickory Limb

The attraction of even a small body of water can be observed any rainy day when young boys feel compelled to wade through every puddle on the way to school. It attracts adults as well. Look at the country real estate ads: "trout stream, river view, beach privileges." In fact, a brook was the reason we bought our farm in Jericho.

The waterfall in the small river that runs through the woods below our house was once the site of one of Mill Brook's five mills. The stream plunges over the rocks and forms a large round pool, seven feet deep at the base of the rocks but tapering off gradually to a gravel beach on the opposite shore. It is about thirty feet by sixty feet and not as cold as you might expect. It meanders through several miles of open pasture just above our place, and this takes out some of the mountain sting. Once we had seen it and knew it was for sale, it had to be ours. The other seventeen acres, house, shed, and two barns were incidental. It is the pool that has pulled us back for twenty-nine summers, and the new house is carefully placed within sight and sound of the waterfall.

When the children were little they took to the water as

naturally as young otters, splashing, cavorting, showing off, and learning to swim because that's what we did and obviously it was fun. We never allowed them to play there alone because I could not see or hear them from the house. My anxiety was only that if one of them, in exploring the rocks, should slip and bang her head, she might knock herself out and fall into the pool. It never occurred to me that a conscious child might be in danger while swimming in a small calm pool. That's what the water is for!

But not all children grow up amphibious. The very first summer Cuy and Enid Hunt, friends from medical school days, came to visit with their three little boys who were two, three, and four years old. Our Debbie was two and a half and Patty was five. So armed with pails and shovels, old sieves, spoons, and toy boats, we all set off for the brook. To my utter amazement the two older boys waded into the water and kept right on walking until it came up over their heads. I expected them to bob up and thrash around. I thought any little animal would struggle for breath, but not the small Hunts! They simply walked under water until I charged in after them and fished little Cuy out while Enid scooped up the next one and headed off the third before he got in that far. I still don't understand it. Would they have just quietly drowned or would the struggle have come at the next moment? We didn't care to find out and urged them to build a dam instead.

One hot July day a few years later, Wally and Ginny Riker and their nine-year-old son Donald, a visiting pharmacologist from India, and an attractive French lady M.D. came for a picnic at the pool. We were all sitting around on the grass talking while the children cavorted in the water. Our girls had a couple of inner tubes that they floated around on and reluctantly shared with Donald after I had fixed them with the evil eye. Nobody mentioned the fact that Donald's experience with water had only been splashing in the surf at Jones Beach and that he couldn't swim.

Suddenly George leaped to his feet, kicked off his loafers, and hurled himself into the water. I looked over towards the waterfall and there were Donald's fingertips fluttering just above the surface. I raced around the pool and jumped in, landing helpfully on top of George and cracking him on the noggin while he was trying to surface dive for Donald. What seemed like minutes later George came up gasping, pulling the boy with him. Fortunately Donald had not inhaled. But he had sunk straight to the bottom. He was grey, limp, and lacking in appetite for some time, but so were we. When he perked up a bit, he told us he had tried to step off from the inner tube to the rocks, but the tube, of course, had bounced out from under him. We made a lot of on-the-spot rules about no tubes for non-swimmers, but of course that situation has never arisen again.

These have been the only close calls in twenty-five years. We have temporarily lost a new pair of shoes, half a bikini, fish hooks, and the contents of an over-loaded hamburger roll but no lives. Once two trout were lost in the pool which sounds ridiculous and it was. Kermit, an obstetrician friend, was—and I suppose still is—an avid trout fisherman. Our pool was one of his regular stops. One day he came galloping back up to the house in his waders and asked for a pail. He showed me what he wanted it for, a dandy twelve-inch brown trout which he wanted to keep alive because he planned to be out a long time. He was rather excited and jubilant, but that is a chronic condition with Kermit so I wasn't alarmed until later when I saw him come dragging up the hill very slowly, set the pail at the corner of the barn, and walk wearily towards his car. Now that was so atypical of hyperkinetic Kermit that I went out to see if he was hurt. His face was so woe-begone that I couldn't laugh when he showed me the empty pail. He had caught two beauties, left them on the grassy bank in the pail half filled with water. But no sooner had he waded out to try for a third when they flipped out of the pail and back into the pool and flirted off downstream in front of the same blue eyes that were almost filling with tears as he told me about it.

But back to hanging your clothes on the hickory limb and avoiding the water. We have no hickories near the pool, but we do have a big old boulder that the children always referred to as the dressing rock. It is tall enough so that an adult can stand behind it with only his head showing. When the girls were tiny they either wore no suits or pulled them on in the open. They watched our guests retire to the semi-privacy of the dressing rock. Soon Patty was imitating the visiting fire-ladies. Debbie wanted to do whatever Patty did so she trotted behind the rock to pull off her small jeans and T-shirt, but she varied the pattern in one aspect. When she emerged from behind the dressing rock and ran into the water, she wore only an oversized bathing cap. When we were ready to go up to the house, she retired behind the rock again to squirm back into her clothes. After all, we called it a dressing rock, didn't we?

Our Woodchuck Would

What's the use of asking how much wood a woodchuck could chuck when the woodchucks of my acquaintance neither could nor would? I've never known a Vermont woodchuck who showed an inclination to even sniff at a piece of wood. What they are wholeheartedly dedicated to is making themselves fat on the fruits, or in our case vegetables, of our labors. After four years of living in a prestigious suburb where no one raised anything edible unless it happened to have a fruit that followed an ornamental flower, we returned to Vermont eager and willing to raise most of the vegetables in the seed catalogues. What I didn't count on was the similarity of the tastes of woodchucks, raccoons, and Wolfs.

We had never fenced in our garden when we lived in Vermont before. But since the eight thousand pine trees we planted have grown twenty feet tall and our pastures have taken to the woods, our animal life has increased in proportion. We had more footprints in our garden than Grauman's Chinese Theater. I have seen deer, rabbits, raccoons, skunks, porcupines, and woodchucks. We also have beaver, but they are busy trying to make a swimming pool bigger than ours.

Besides, they prefer wood. So do the porcupines. If this had happened our first year back, we would have fenced the garden. At least I hope we would have gotten the message from our furry friends. It would be nice to believe that we have not outgrown some learning ability. But we were misled, being granted a season of grace. We returned in May, planted twenty-five varieties of vegetables, and watched them grow unmolested by anything bigger than striped cucumber beetles until the raccoons preempted the corn crop in late August. But fencing would not have kept the raccoons out anyway. Do you know anything that does? We have neighbors who have hidden their sweet corn in the middle of six acres of field to no avail. They can go over, under, and around any of the usual barriers. Pig wire just serves as a jungle gym for their children. Folklore to the contrary, I have not found them deterred by blood meal, kerosene, or moth balls. The things that are supposed to scare deer such as tin cans or aluminum plates swinging in the breeze simply make the garden more entertaining to a raccoon family, a variation of the Tivoli Gardens with something for all ages. In a fit of frustration that summer I wrapped some of the nearly ripe ears of corn in aluminum foil fastened with rubber bands, but they were unwrapped and eaten.

If we had had a coon dog and a man willing to spend every night patrolling the garden, that probably would have discouraged the raccoons. But we didn't have a dog, and the man of this house was willing to make rounds but not stay on duty all night.

So raccoons seemed hopeless, or more accurately, raising corn on our land seemed hopeless. Maybe we should have raised raccoons. Could the vogue for Daniel Boone hats and coonskin coats be revived? You are welcome to that idea if it appeals to you because it wouldn't be practical here. We would be drummed out of the Jericho town meeting if we did anything to encourage a raccoon population explosion.

What concerned me was how to get the woodchucks to share the peas and beans with us. It was a question of who had more would—we or the woodchucks. It was a contest of wills. The only trouble was that, although I am bigger and I used to think I was smarter, they were the ones who were enjoying the vegetables. You see they preferred the early leaves of the peas and beans, and I have been conditioned to prefer the fruits. That gave them a month's head start. In fact, there wouldn't be any fruits if they kept eating the leaves, tendrils, and blossoms. I tried to discourage them with applications of blood meal and rotenone. The rain washed those off. Marigolds are supposed to repel cabbage worms and nematodes, so I planted marigolds in the garden. For a while I thought the woodchucks shared my distaste for the smell of marigolds, but one night they ate the marigolds, too.

In desperation we covered half the garden with sheets of plastic at night and put buckets over the cabbages. I doubted that they would overturn the pails, but we soon realized they could creep under the plastic if they felt like it. The sleeker and fatter they became, the leaner, or at least the hungrier, I grew. I took to mumbling in front of vegetable stands, ripping seed catalogues in half with my bare hands, and hating my neighbors whose gardens were unmolested.

The handwriting on the tool shed wall was all too clear. We fenced the garden. That separated the Wolfs from the wild for one season, but either the old woodchucks grew wiser or the younger generation was more enterprising because the following year one of them dug a hole under the fence and feasted on broccoli. George found an old spring trap in the barn and set that near the hole. The next day, armed with a roll of chicken wire and twistems, I bent the chicken wire and fastened it all along the bottom of the fence and one foot out into the grass. I crawled along on my knees twisting it firmly every few inches. I forgot one thing. A loud snap and a very restraining piece of metal pinned my left hand to the ground and jogged my memory. I tried to release the trap with my right hand—not strong enough. I tried to get my foot on the trap—wouldn't reach. Fortunately it was Saturday and George was home, so I did the womanly thing and wailed like a banshee. No need to elaborate on his opinion of someone who catches herself in her own trap!

At that point our woodchuck would have chucked me right onto a psychiatrist's couch except for the knowledge that psychiatric treatment for paranoia is not covered by our medical insurance.

Did the double fence keep the woodchuck at bay? It did. And a battery-powered electric wire six inches above the fence gave us a respite from the raccoons and bountiful harvests for two years.

But last summer, just as the corn was almost ready to pick and we were snuggled all safe in our beds, the raccoons chose shock rather than self-denial and decimated the crop.

Don't suggest planting pumpkins or beans among the corn rows. We've done that. Ditto for red pepper and a lamp burning all night. Don't tell me we should have a dog. I'd have to take care of him all year, and I only have to fret about raccoons for one month.

It's a non-lethal form of Russian roulette, but maybe that's the challenge. It's a new game every year. Will the woodchucks beat the Wolfs next season? Will the Wolfs outwit the masked bandits in the corn patch? Join us for the next installment of this bucolic soap opera to be continued in 1980, 1981, and until death, preferably theirs, doth us part.

Why Can't a Man
Be More like a Woman?

I like men. In fact if I were stranded on a desert island with only one person, I would certainly prefer a male companion. I am sure that he would be better than I at cracking open coconuts and weaving a palm-leaf thatch.

But why can't a man be more like a woman? I'm not just talking about husbands. I've only had one and that hardly qualifies as scientific research. But I also have had one father, two sons-in-law, and a fairly wide, if not intimate, acquaintance with other males too numerous to mention. And while they vary in age, size, and previous condition of servitude, there are certain idiosyncrasies that, for better or worse, are different from women.

I began to suspect that the difference between men and women was more than anatomical when I was ten years old and my father bought his first car. We spent the summers in Maine and the trip from Montclair, New Jersey, to central Maine, which took three days, gave me my first intimations of the differences between the sexes. My mother did all the in-door packing, including a telescoping wicker hamper for bedding, an enormous duffle bag, assorted suitcases, and bizarre-shaped bundles of lares and penates. But the instant these impedimenta were outside the door, it was a man's prerogative to pack the car. We had a Studebaker touring car with a folding luggage rack on the side. It also had isinglass curtains which were stored conveniently under the back seat. When the heavens unloaded, the occupants of the back seat had to get out and stand in the rain while the irate male parent removed the pile of bags and boxes wedged between my sister and me as a deterrent to internecine warfare, lifted out the seat, and unearthed the curtains. The salesman had said that these curtains snapped easily into place. He lied. It took much more strength of arm and vocabulary than a ten-year-old possessed. In fact my father was known to go so far as to call their inventor a "darned fool" and "confounded idiot." Strong language in our household where "to raise one's voice" was to be "ordinary" was a cardinal sin. My mother's reaction to upsetting a bowl of gravy all over the damask tablecloth was "how provoking!"

Then there was at least one, perhaps more, flat tire per day which meant total decampment at the side of the road while father mended the inner tube with red rubber patches, pumped it up by hand, and put the tire back together again. This took long enough to allow me to wander into the field to pick daisies or to collect stones to add to the small cairn I was building on my side of the car's floor. I preferred that to listening to father moan. In fact, I would have preferred to be sent on ahead by train—especially since I was already in disfavor because I had opened the rear door of the car on my side forgetting that the luggage rack was on that side, and when that door was opened, it required Herculean strength to shut it again.

But the major and universal difference between men and women, impressed on me in those early years and still true today, is attitude towards asking directions. My mother sat on the front seat holding *The Blue Book* on her lap. In the days before highway maps and route (pronounced "rout") numbers, *The Blue Book* could tell you how to get from Montclair to wherever you chose. Turn right at the white church in Suffern. But if the road to the right was unpaved my father preferred to stay on the macadam road and did so. This resulted in a lot of retracking through the back streets. At that point my mother would want to ask for directions, even as you and I would. But "he" (your father, husband or son-in-law) prefers to wander up hill and down dale rather than lose face by admitting he is hopelessly lost.

Even the tender loving care given us by the police in Switzerland only convinced my husband that that was the exception to his rule, that directions given by a native are misleading, incorrect, or both. We were driving through Switzerland and planning to spend the night at the Novotel near Neuchatel. As we approached Neuchatel there was road construction and a detour. Nothing daunted George who proceeded through the city and out the other side until it became obvious that we were almost in France. So we turned around and drove back through the city and out the other side several miles. No sign of the Novotel. But suddenly I saw a police barracks and was able to persuade George to stop with the understanding that I would do the asking.

The door was locked. It was a Sunday, but there was a police car in front which I didn't think had gotten there by itself. So I pulled the bell, and way down the corridor I could see a small figure running towards me. My college French was adequate to make my request known to the gendarme who opened the door, but it was not enough for me to follow the flood of his Gallic and dramatic instructions. So he screamed for Pierre who also catapulted down the hall pulling on his jacket. With a great swoop of his doffed cap he ushered me through the door, bowed, and with a "Suivez-moi" leapt into the waiting police car and led us triumphantly to the motel with lights flashing and brakes screeching. He never braked at the entrance but doffed his cap again and was off into the foggy night.

The next area of differentiation is that women enjoy shopping for clothes. Men don't. In fact, they won't do it unless they are dragged protesting and muttering along the pavement. Have you ever gone shopping with your husband in a *haute couture* haberdashery? Don't. Men have certain tribal rites that no woman would dream of performing. First comes the stand off. Your husband looks as though he can't imagine how he happens to be there and certainly has no idea why. The salesman continues his conversation with another salesman and examines his molar in the mirror. After a decent interval there is the encounter in which the salesman addresses you, not your husband, with "Something in a suit, today?" Now the only things *in* a suit are your husband in his shiny old threads and the salesman in his skin-tight pinstripe. Mercifully neither are for sale. But he proceeds to the evaluation.

"Let's see. You are about a 38 short." He never asks. He announces, and it is always a size to make a fat man feel fatter, a short man feel like a midget, and a thin man prepare his will. There is a feint at fitting. He wedges a jacket out of the rack saying, "We'll just try this on for size." The sleeves hang well below your husband's fingertips and the bottom of the jacket envelops his knees. "A touch roomy, perhaps?" The racks are of course off limits to the buyer. He presumably doesn't know his size or preference. By now he doesn't know his name, rank, or serial number and looks retarded. The salesman pulls out two more suits, and they are invariably green and purple. If your husband mutters, "I was thinking of Oxford grey," he will be told that they are not selling that this season. "You don't want an old-looking suit, do you?"

Oh he doesn't, eh? That is just what he does want, and he is already inside it. At this point you fear that they will both be disappointed, but with the knowledge that he won't be able to buy a suit that day, your husband straightens up, assumes his dignity and intelligence, and sails out of the store, with you in tow, grinning as though he had just been rescued from the teeth of Jaws II.

Another area is lost and found. "Where did you put my torque wrench?" or "Where's that flannel shirt that I wore on the canoe trip up the Allagash in 1948?" Hardly items that you would purloin for your own use even if you knew how to use them. Do you ever ask your husband where he put your pantyhose? Of course not. And if he finds his misplaced treasure does he tell you? No, you spend the next hour upside down in the closet, and when you finally back out and admit defeat, he cheerfully announces, "Oh, I found it half an hour ago."

When you promised to cherish him in sickness and in health did anyone point out to you the difference between his sickness and yours? And a husband with an M.D. after his name is even worse because he knows all the awful things he could get.

When we were first married and George was a senior medical student, he came home one day and crept into bed half clothed and weighted down by ten pounds of Cecil's *Textbook of Medicine*. He was convinced that he had meningitis and that his hours were numbered. A little later he dragged himself into the bathroom and looked at his face in the mirror. "German measles," he shrieked happily. "What's for dinner?" But when one morning I complained of a pain under my ear, his sympathetic remark was "There's nothing wrong with you. Go on to school, you old crock." I was a nursery school teacher, and when I entered the school hall, the school doctor took one look at me and said, "You've got mumps. Get out of here before you infect the kids. Didn't you say your husband was almost through medical school?"

When it comes to treatment of his ailments, the M.D. husband wouldn't dream of consulting a colleague. He looks up the side effects of an appropriate drug and decides against taking it. George had suffered from a foot infection for more than a year before we left for Finland to visit our daughter. George yearned to try a real Finnish sauna but politely refused the invitations from Finnish friends lest he contaminate their saunas. So Patty suggested he go to the sauna in the hotel where the floors were scrubbed and disinfected daily. She made the arrangements on the house phone in Finnish, gave George a few instructions, and sent him on his way. When he entered the sauna suite, a lady asked him something in Finnish, and George nodded vigorously assuming that she was asking if he was the man whose daughter had just called. He went into the sauna, took off his clothes, sat in the sauna until he was convinced that death was imminent, came out, went back in, and when he emerged for the second time a very large lady in a white uniform beckoned him towards her. She flipped him neatly down on a table and with the dispatch of an English nanny proceeded to scrub him from head to toe. Now George is a very modest man. In an agony of embarrassment he resorted to the only help at his disposal. He shut *his* eyes. So he was unprepared for the bucket of cold water she sloshed over him. Ignoring his gasp, she expertly turned him over and attacked his other side with determination. This time he opened his eyes to anticipate the deluge and caught it full in the face. Then she motioned him up. He stood up. She shook her head. He lay down. She shook her head. Communication was at a standstill so she picked him up, sat him on the edge of the table, and shampooed his hair with enough enthusiasm to uncurl Medusa's locks. Finally he was allowed to escape, and he fled to his suddenly beloved clothes.

By the time his gelatinous knees got him back down to the hotel room, he was still red-faced and making strange whinnying noises somewhere between laughter and tears. Patty attributed it to the sauna, but George protested that it was from embarrassment and regaled us with his story.

"Then why did you agree to have a scrub lady?" Patty asked.

"Is *that* what she asked me? I was just trying to be agreeable and improve the American image."

Now a woman would have fled or protested or both. Or she would have decided that it was just another ethnic experience and would have thought it funny. Oddly enough only two of us thought George's sauna was funny.

It is not always easy for a woman to understand the machinations of the male mind. But what woman wants to understand everything? When it comes to filling out the income tax forms, deciphering a legal document, solving the riddle of strange noises in the car's engine, or tender loving care when things go bump in the night—Ah Men!

What Do You Mean, Birdbrain?

You've probably never asked a real estate agent if the house he is showing you is in a good bird neighborhood. Just as well. He wouldn't be likely to tell you if it was in the center of a plague of starlings anyhow. The average prospective buyer is more concerned with mortgages than whether or not a house is on the north-south flyway.

If you are a city dweller you are apt to tolerate or ignore the ubiquitous English sparrows, starlings, or pigeons. But a country person hopes for bird neighbors whose habits and family life are congenial with his. Our phoebe couple, who returned every year to join us in—or as near as they could get into—our old house in Jericho, were so much a part of our life there that the question and answer, "Phoebe?" "Phoebe," evoked the image and smell of Jericho no matter where we heard it.

I admired the cardinal couple who honored us with their presence on the stone terrace of our big house in Kansas City, but they were more formal than the phoebes. They never chatted about their anxieties and enthusiasms the way the phoebes did. And I resented the way the female meekly waited until the male was through eating before she dared take a sunflower seed. True he offered her a seed now and then rather gallantly, but you got the impression that they were his seeds to dispense or withold according to his whim.

The pigeons who lived up around the tall chimneys on our slate roof in Kansas were only a nuisance. There were so many of them that sitting on the terrace was a risky business. Besides, despite their sleek appearance they were terrible home builders and housekeepers. Even if I didn't delight in the brilliant coloring of Baltimore orioles, I would still admire their skill in weaving a pouch of grass, string, and horsehair suspended from the tips of elm branches. But the pigeons just kick together a few scraps of trash, a twig or two, or bits of leaves on any old exposed ledge on a building. The nest has no cup shape so the eggs roll out frequently and crash to the ground. One not very bright mother pigeon in Kansas City twice laid her eggs right in the rain gutter under our bedroom window so with each thunderstorm the nest, eggs, and mama were awash with cold rain water. Those eggs never hatched, of course, but I doubt if she ever wondered why.

Some birds, however, not only take tender loving care of their own families but occasionally act in *loco parentis* to unrelated species. There was the cardinal who took it upon herself to feed the goldfish in an outdoor pool in North Carolina. She would chirp till the goldfish gathered at the edge of the pool and then bring food for them exactly as if she was stuffing a brood of her own.

The blue jay, much maligned because of his rowdy ways and preemption of the feeder, undergoes a personality change during the nesting season. High in a pine tree next to our house I noticed that one jay sat on a limb while another brought it tidbits, whistled soft endearments, and then flew off for more. After a few days of courtship they built a nest.

While she sat on the nest, the male bird brought her food, but he never flew directly to the nest. He would alight on a lower branch and then hop upwards, circling the tree trunk limb by limb till he reached the nest. After the eggs were hatched both parents flew a shuttle fast-food service but always approached the nest by the invisible circular staircase. Neither of them ever squawked, screamed, or sounded the jay alarm during this period. They were as docile and furtive as hermit thrushes.

I have seen cardinals spill seeds almost intentionally so that the ground-feeding small birds, like tree sparrows or redpolls, could pick them up. These cardinals weren't just careless and clumsy like the evening grosbeaks we have in Jericho. They scattered a few seeds, looked down at the small birds, ate some, looked down again, and, if the supply on the ground was gone, scattered some more.

We had a female grouse, or "patridge" as it is known in these parts, who kept us under house arrest, perhaps defending a nest or a brood we never knew. I'm not sure the little ones existed except in her instincts because she spent all her time keeping us in line. She would attack either one of us when we came out the door, hurl herself against the hub caps of the car, and glare at us through the picture window if we cowered indoors.

Everyone with a bird feeder is familiar with the pecking order among the different birds. We once had a small South American Araucana hen given to us by the poultryman at the University. She was immediately assigned to the bottom rung on the social totem pole in our henhouse. She had to wait to eat until the domestic hens had filled their crops and was pushed to the farthest and coldest spot on the roost at night.

If a baby chick ever got through the fence between the chicks' brooder and the laying hens' quarters, the old girls

rushed at it and would peck it to death in seconds if we didn't scoop it up.

But all birdbrains are not avian. I was dismayed by a tale of human prejudice told to me by a friend in North Dakota. A neighbor of his saw a large unfamiliar bird in a tree in her backyard and decided it had an ominous look. She phoned the police who came at once, agreed that the bird was unusual, and promptly shot it. When our friend arrived on the scene quite a crowd had gathered around the *corpus delecti*, a handsome pileated woodpecker. He was aghast, not only that the bird was dead but that everyone in the group was praising the policeman for his wisdom in protecting the neighborhood from dangerous birds.

"Why did you shoot it?" he asked. "It's a harmless pileated woodpecker that is getting so rare that we should be protecting it from extinction."

"Why did I shoot it? Because it looked different, that's why. If it had looked like a regular woodpecker I would have left it alone, but with that long beak and red pointed head it didn't look like any bird I knew. I figure we don't want any *strange* looking birds around here."

Try "Open Sesame" on Your Pill Bottle

Whatever happened to all that time saved by "convenience" foods and "improved" packaging? Every housewife and an increasing number of househusbands can tell you the answer to that one. It is spent in trying to unscrew, poke, or blast out the contents of those packages without completely destroying the food, catapulting the pills under the dishwasher, or breaking fingernails and the Sabbath with undeleted expletives.

The ulcer patient may see through a package of antacid tablets and admire the way they are laminated in rows between a layer of foil on the back and little plastic bubbles on the front; but in the time it takes him to penetrate the foil or poke through the plastic bubbles with the letter-opener, his gastric juices are responding to his rage, and his ulcer is protesting painfully. So he gives up and dashes to the kitchen for a glass of milk and a ham sandwich only to find that in the time it takes him to pull the little red tag on the package of sliced ham, which comes off in his hand, and to try to slip a knife under the plexiglass dome that is programmed to keep the ham in isolation as long as possible, he could have cooked, carved, and trimmed a conventional ham to his specifications. He might even have had time to raise the pig instead of his blood pressure. And not everyone is adept at opening the spout on milk containers either. The layers of waxed cardboard have a habit of separating, and there he'll be kept at a respectful distance from the milk for another thirty seconds.

The plastic skin that is sealed onto fresh meat is fixed for life, yours or the shelf life of the meat, whichever comes first. You can't just unfold it like the butcher wrap of my youth. You have to claw your way in until the wrap suddenly loses its muscle tone and shrinks into a limp scrap. No wonder we've become addicted to fast foods. Cooking at home has literally become cooking from scratch.

From early youth I've approached a sardine can with the knowledge that (a) the key may be missing, (b) the key may refuse to engage the metal lip, (c) the top may only peel back in a tiny triangle granting a half-inch view of the sardines, or (d) you find that the can won't fit on your electric can opener. Back to the hand can opener, the jagged edge, and the spilled oil that only your cat finds attractive.

Not all the diabolic inventive genius has been directed towards food. How about the new safety pill boxes? Their noble purpose is to prevent children from getting their hands on the pills. But a raccoon is potentially more capable of solving the problem than the average adult. The raccoon and many of our children can't read. It says "open," arrow pointing left, and "close," arrow to the right. It also says "push down while turning," but it doesn't tell you that you have to set the bottle on a firm table and *lean* on it. The child whose natural habitat is the floor has the advantage. I tried one bottle with my hands for three minutes before I set it down and bore down with the full weight of my frustration.

I have an elderly friend with a severe tremor. It is impossible for her to open a safety bottle, and she must ask a neighbor to set out a week's supply of medications on her sideboard where they are much more accessible to visiting grandchildren than in a conventional bottle on the bathroom shelf.

No wonder those bottles are made out of plastic! At least when frustration prompts you to hurl one across the room it won't break like a glass bottle, adding lacerations to your list of chief complaints.

If I were a cardiac patient and had faith that a nitroglycerin tablet, at the first twinge of angina, might keep me on the earthly side of the pearly gates, my panic would accelerate in proportion to the length of time I spent in fumbling with the pill bottle. Perhaps angina is not an everyday occurrence, but a lot of doctors prescribe the tranquilizer diazepam, and have you ever tried to get at those pills?

I'd love to believe that we are evolving into a society of stoic, if not always healthy, souls who cope without medications, but the statistics show that the opposite is true. Average consumers expect all the illnesses and paliatives or remedies that the literature tells them they should have.

The obvious conclusion is that we are installing self-opening garage doors, self-cleaning ovens, and self-defrosting refrigerators and are using pre-cooked foods so that we can devote the time saved to cracking the code of the very private world of packaging.

In Praise of Pigs

Never underestimate the power of a pig or the persuasion of a pig fancier. We bought our first pigs in 1949 when we were only summer Vermonters, and we had to have them dressed off at the tender age of five and a half months so that we could take our hams and pork back to New York City. I blush to admit that I was scared to death of those two squealing six-week-old little blimps and begged the daughter of the neighbor from whom we bought them to ride home with me and help me get them settled in their pen.

That was thirty years and forty pigs ago. There were ten years when we lived "away" in Weston, Massachusetts, and Mission Hills, Kansas, except for a month in Vermont each summer. If you are familiar with either of those suburbs, you know we didn't keep pigs there. Our small vegetable garden was even considered a blot on the landscape.

But when we came back to Vermont for good, pigs were high on our list of priorities. Why are we so enthusiastic about pigs? Because they are the easiest, most cheerful, and brightest animals out of the collection that we've had over the years which included turkeys, ducks, chickens, sheep, rabbits, one goat, one horse, many cats, and two dogs. And don't tell me again about your horse who could find his way home or your golden retriever's sensitivity to your moods. It's not that I don't believe you. It's just that we are more comfort oriented now. We no longer have a horse or a dog, and we intend to keep it that way. We used to enjoy the cats, or more specifically the kittens, but they spent most of their days and nights in the fields or the barn. Our odd theory is that our animals should be productive members of the establishment rather than parasites. The horse that we had for three years was eighty percent trouble and only twenty percent transportation and recreation combined. And now that I no longer have to change diapers, keep immunization records, and fish yard-long hairs out of the shower drains, why should I revert to those chores for a dog? I'll admit it is not a popular attitude, and I overheard a friend remark sadly, "You see they're not dog people. They're more, well, ah, pig people."

I was flattered when the grain salesman referred to me as the "pig lady." If I could maintain the wholehearted dedication that is built into every pig I've known, I would have written a hundred books instead of five and my house and garden would look like the magazine of the same name.

Pigs don't whine in the night, tangle with porcupines or skunks, roll in dead woodchucks, or expect to be part of the family. Can you say that for your dog? We've never had one in the parlor or in a poke either. We get two at six weeks and feed them twice a day. It is a pleasure to see them cavort around their pen and to pat their solid living hams. And after feeding them you can just go on about your business without a moment's concern for their psyches.

Pigs are cleaner than any other farm animal except the cat. Your dog and cat may be housebroken, and I certainly hope they are, but what about your horse, cows, sheep, and chickens who go through life casually relieving themselves when and where they get the urge? If our pigpen is dirty, and it often is, it is our fault and not the pigs'. Pigs will choose one corner of their quarters for sanitary purposes, another spot for sleeping, and another for eating even as you and I would with our illusions of civilized behavior. They can look muddy because in hot weather they enjoy getting their skins wet, especially if no shade has been provided for them.

We have never attempted to butcher our pigs ourselves. We had neither the stomach nor the know-how for it, and so when they were six months old or weighed over two hundred pounds, whichever came first, we loaded them into whatever pig-proof vehicle we had at the moment and transported them to the nearest meat packing company.

But the last two years we have enjoyed the services of Andy Abair of Barre and Ted Alexander of Jericho. Mr. Abair looks like Longfellow's blacksmith and comes in a truck which contains a bathtub, a water heater, an enormous tripod, a gun, scrapers, and knives. He sets up the tripod on the grass in front of the barn, fills the water heater and fires it up, strolls into the pig pen, shoots the pig, slits its throat, and hangs it from the tripod, all very quick and relatively untraumatic to the owners especially since I stay in the house until he has reached that point. Then he eviscerates the pig, lowers it into the filled bathtub, and scrapes off the bristles.

Our barn is close to the road, and the first time Mr. Abair came was a Sunday afternoon with the usual Sunday drivers tooling along our back road enjoying the lilacs and apple blossoms. Their bucolic reveries were suddenly interrupted. Brakes screeched or cars accelerated according to the reactions of the occupants who stared in horror or amusement at the sight of one large pig hanging by his hind legs from the tripod and the other enormous pink porker reclining in the bathtub with her head and forefeet spilling over the edge of the tub, exactly as Miss Piggy would look in her beauty bath.

Mr. Abair is a no-nonsense craftsman, all work and no small talk. And he doesn't consider himself a Sunday sideshow. One neighbor from whom we had bought these pigs drove past, stopped, and came over to watch.

"How much do you charge?"

No answer.

"How much do you get for doing this?"

No answer.

Bob turned to me and whispered, "You ask him."

After a decent interval I explained that Bob also raised pigs and wanted to get an idea of his price.

Mr. Abair went on scraping bristles and, addressing the pig, said, "Depends."

I learned later that it does depend—on how many pigs, how far he has to travel, and whether or not there are others in the vicinity on the same day. The day he had butchered ours he had done four in Underhill and was going to do two more in Richmond. He spent only an hour and a half at our place including setting up the tripod, filling and heating the hot water tank, shooting, bleeding and eviscerating the pigs, scraping off the bristles, and cutting the carcasses in half.

After he left we took the four halves, now in the back of our truck, into Jericho Center to Ted Alexander's custom butchering establishment where he hung our meat in his cooler.

Have you ever tried to handle half of a fresh-killed pig? Rigor mortis has not set in, and the carcass is soft and flexible and seems to weigh twice its actual weight. It slips, slides, and brings you to your knees. But once the cooler door shut on our meat, all we had to do was come back in a few days to pick it up cut, wrapped, labeled, and ready for the freezer.

Of course I might not look with such favor on pigs if we did all the butchering, rendered lard, and made such unappealing (to me) dishes as blood pudding and headcheese. I do render a small amount of lard, and we feed the rest of the fat to the birds who seem to consider it as tasty as beef suet. Even with total grain feeding and paying for the butchering, the cost of our pork is way below that in the supermarket, and the product is far superior.

So on a yearly basis we enjoy the pigs for six months on the hoof and for another six months in the freezer. The manure goes on the garden. George even mutters periodically about the possible uses of pigskin. I haven't given up buying shoes or gloves yet, but don't forget what I said about the persuasion of a pig person! You may yet hear the tap-tap-tap of a cobbler's hammer on Nashville Road.

Heard Any Good
News Lately?

Are you as tired as I am of perversion, pornography, and pot? Sick of reading about hold-ups, drop-outs and sit-ins? Think about it for a minute. How many abnormal, criminal, or alarming things have really happened to you or members of your family in the last six months? Now how many reassuring, kind-hearted, laugh-provoking incidents involved your family during the same period?

Surprising isn't it? The good moments, the kindnesses, the funny experiences outnumber the few bad episodes by such a large proportion that it makes you wonder why that isn't reflected in our press and in our conversation.

The fact is that most people are not bad at all. We don't live in a ghetto or belong to a minority group, but our family is not isolated from problems. But do you really want to hear about them? Of course not. I'm boring you just by mentioning them. I'm boring myself, too. It's much more interesting to tell and listen to the good things that happen to you.

When our twenty-three-year-old daughter became ill in London on her way from Yugoslavia to the United States, she didn't know what was wrong with her; and she only knew one person in London, a boy who had been in the same international work camp with Patty in Norway. She phoned him for advice, and he and his mother took one look at her and hurried her to their home. Elsie Barton had never seen Patty before, and what a bedraggled sight she was—jaundiced, disheveled, and carrying all her worldly goods in a backpack. But at considerable inconvenience and risk to her own family, Mrs. Barton gave Patty the priceless healing prescription, tender loving care. She nursed a very sick Patty through hepatitis for a month until she was strong enough to make the trip home. Now, THAT never made the papers.

After graduating from college, our younger daughter Debbie went off to New York to seek her fortune. On one of her first days of foot-weary job hunting she sat in a bus next to a girl who dropped a nickel on the floor. The girl started to pick it up, but stopped and said, "No, I'll leave it. Think how good it will make somebody feel to find it!"

Within two weeks Debbie had both a job and a shared apartment, but because of the high cost of living in New York, she was somewhat less than affluent. By the time she paid for the rent, utilities, food, and bus fare she had very little left to squander on furbelows. A new dress was a considerable investment. One day she made such an investment in a small dress shop, walked across the street to a five-and-ten-cent-store, put the dress box down on the counter to examine something, and when she looked up her dress box was gone! (The evil city. You can't trust anyone.) She sadly went back across the street to the dress shop. When she started to tell her sad tale one large tear ran down her cheek, and the saleslady urged her to go back to the five-and-ten and tell them about it. She did, and as she described the box half expecting a bored reaction, the sales girl said, "Wait a minute," reached under the counter, and pulled out Debbie's dress box! She went back across the street again with her box and good news, and the original saleslady burst into happy tears and the manager threw his arms around Debbie and hugged her. (Hard-hearted city. No one cares.)

Not caring has supposedly come to the country, too. Everyone is supposed to be too busy for little acts of kindness. In Jericho one summer when we used canned gas for cooking fuel, we ran out of one tank and were low on the other. I phoned Steve's Home Supply in Essex Junction eight miles away, and the girl said she would put us down on the list for delivery. A few days later and with the 4th of July weekend coming up we were again in Essex Junction and stopped to see if there was any way to expedite delivery. Steve, the owner, who had been in business there ever since he came through town as a Champlain Valley Fair roustabout more than forty years ago was standing in the driveway. I told him our predicament.

"You and everybody else. We've got about a hundred deliveries to make. We'll do the best we can, but we're swamped."

We were hardly home when Steve and his wife drove into our yard in their own truck. George thanked him for making a special trip, and Steve said, "Well Doc, I couldn't *not* do it. I remember when your kids and mine were little. It's been a long time."

A neighbor, Isabella Martin, told me another heart-warmer. She had stopped for gas at Desso's, the village store in Jericho Center, filled the tank herself, paid for the gas, and, in the confusion of corraling her two little boys and stuffing them and the groceries into the car, had set her pocketbook on the roof of the car. She drove off, never giving the purse another thought until she got home. She couldn't remember where she had mislaid it and drove back to the store. No luck. It was not on Desso's counter either.

Some days later, Lillian Desso phoned to say that an unidentified skiier had brought the pocketbook into the store. He had found it somewhere along Brown's Trace and thought Lillian might know the owner. And by now what was inside the pocketbook? Everything! Money, credit cards, and the assorted bits and pieces of lares and penates that stuff a young mother's pocketbook.

A nice surprise happened during our last spring in Kansas. On May 26, the eighty-third birthday of Louise Andrews Kent, who is known in these parts as Mrs. Appleyard, author and Rennaissance lady of multiple talents, Mrs. Kent sent me a copy of the beautiful new book *Vermont: A Special World*. Now how many people do you know who send gifts to others on their own birthdays?

Yesterday I received an envelope in the mail from the postmaster in a nearby town. I had bought some stamps there two days before, paid for them, but left them on the counter. Before I had noticed they were missing, they arrived in the mail. That postmaster doesn't know me from Eve. I had mailed a package at the same time; and when he saw I had left the stamps, he looked among the packages until he found mine, copied off the return address, and sent the stamps to me. He could have just held the stamps until I noticed my carelessness and returned. He could also have dropped them back in the drawer and pocketed the money. But he didn't. That's what I like about Vermont!

Tell Me Not in Mournful Numbers

If all the numbers in the world were placed end to end around the center of the earth, I'd rather you called it the equator. I answer to my name not to my social security number, not because I am perverse but because I haven't the slightest idea what my social security number is. I do carry it with me—unless it is in my other pocketbook along with the numbers for my hospital identification card, library card, six credit cards, two checking accounts, two savings accounts, and safe deposit box—only because I am tired of having people look at me as though I am retarded. I have no recent proof that I am not, but who wants to be reminded of personal flaws? Nobody glares at me because I wear glasses, have two teeth that did not grow where they are now, and have my hair touched up.

Am I really expected to remember that to the Fletcher Free Library I am 26199, the Medical Center thinks of me fondly as 532-3787, while the Sears Roebuck salesman—who doesn't look a bit brighter than I—is disappointed that I don't rattle off 3-82231-34399-5 when he asks my credit card number? If the numbers inside my savings account passbook ran into as many figures as that I'd be a billionaire. But can you believe that my license runs into quadrillions? And the one I had in Kansas had even one more digit. It's no wonder that the man at the Department of Motor Vehicles called out, "Lady in the blue coat." You could hardly expect him to sing out "W 15442835212542314."

I admit that the word *glycosylhydroxylysine*, which I saw just now in the newspaper, is three letters longer and just as incomprehensible to me, but the accompanying photograph of two medical researchers involved in its production implied that it is not a household article. You might spend a lifetime without ever hearing the word, and I hope you do, but most of us between the ages of sixteen and eighty-six are regular paying customers of the Department of Motor Vehicles.

The only cheerful thing I noticed in shuffling those cards so that I could copy down these numbers is that my dependent identification number is the same as my social security number. I thought it looked familiar, which shows I don't have total amnesia. It's just that when those blank-faced girls behind desks in offices ask me for it, all I can say is, "Well, it is divided in three parts, like Gaul, and the first part starts with an O." That's not the way to build an enduring relationship.

I do remember my age, not because I want to but because few of us have ages that have more than two digits. And that's part of the whole problem with numbers—there are too many of them and they are too long. There is a memory test used in psychiatric evaluations in which the patient is asked to repeat seven digits. The only reason I have passed as legally sane this long is that no one ever got around to testing me. I probably couldn't remember my own telephone number if it wasn't divided. But if the telephone company installs so many phones that the numbers will have to have four sections like that go-around for out-of-town information where you dial the area code number and then 1-555-1212, it will cut down on my out-going phone calls—which might not be a bad idea.

I'm glad I was never in the armed services, not because I am a conscientious objector but because I've been spared a serial number to forget. I am also glad I went to college when at least a few members of the faculty knew at least some of the students' names. In fact, we didn't have numbers at all. You were known by name and face; after you heard the roll call a few times you linked up the names and faces without even trying.

If there must be marks in school, I prefer letters to numbers. Nothing beats the look of an "A" on a term paper. Of course nothing is more depressing than an "F" either, but there is no doubt about what it means.

I wouldn't outlaw numbers altogether. The number concept is essential. A check for $100 makes a lot of sense, and a bill for $30 every time the car opens its hood and says "Ah" at the service station conveys a definite if dreary message. When you are planning a dinner party, it makes a big difference in your day if you know whether to expect six or sixty. And when I get the flu, I'm not satisfied to know simply that I have a temperature. I want to know how much so that I will know how sick to feel. You would be surprised at the difference in your product if you put four teaspoons of baking powder in a cake instead of two. But can you imagine shopping if you had to remember that tuna fish was marked Z-3405 instead of by Copenhagen's little mermaid? How would you recognize Aunt Jemima if she were 8304-7256? There is no hint of her familiar face in those numbers. Why do you suppose numbers are used for codes on the bottom of packages like cottage cheese? So the average housewife can't tell if it is fresh or not. And that is just what is troubling me, not only the freshness of the cottage cheese but of me. I feel I am losing my identity, not only by being a number but because I am a different number to Texaco, the U.S. Government, and the local bank. It would at least lighten my pocketbook if my social security number could be used for all the varied services. With a bit of effort I should be able to master that one series of numbers. But I'm going to cling to my name instead of my number in as many areas as possible.

I'm not campaigning for Ms. or my maiden name. I'm delighted to be my husband's wife—and I hope he likes the arrangement too, but I'm sure he doesn't want to be married to 098-03-2396.

You'd have a hard time selling a car by its serial number or promoting a book by its Library of Congress numerals. And what would be the fun of writing an article if you couldn't indulge in the narcissism of seeing your name on it? I have no illusions that my words are immortal, but they are my words and no one else would have put them together in just that way. For a longer or shorter life span they are my imprint on the sands of time, and I have no intention of sharing either the criticism or the kudos with 098-03-2396.

Who's Sheepish Now?

Noah had the right idea. Animals belong in pairs. Of course what he had in mind was procreation. What we have in mind is recreation with the ultimate goal of consumption.

A dog-loving friend once said to me in disgust, "You only raise animals that you can eat!" Quite true and I made no apologies. What's wrong with that as long as I don't bring our pigs into her living room or harbor any inclination to eat her dogs?

The only animals that ever caused us more frustration than gratification were two dogs and a horse. And each of those lived with us as a singleton. Now I can't guarantee that if we'd had two horses, our old lady horse would have been less ornery or that if we'd had two cockers, our Ginger would not have been consumed with wanderlust, but the fact remains that our two geese waddle around on their outsize webbed feet as though guided by a central radar. Our two sheep are inseparable and our two pigs spend a lot of time in conversation with each other. I suppose each one of our seventeen laying hens would mutter and cackle as much alone as she does in concert, but we've never considered keeping a solitary hen.

How do you divide one fried egg between two people?

We like to watch our livestock, but we're more interested in what they do with each other than how they act toward us. That separates the pet people from the food producers. A dog person wants his pet to love, honor, and obey him till death doth them part. We have no illusions that the enthusiasm with which the pigs greet us each morning is based on anything but hunger pangs. Of course it's nice to be noticed and it is gratifying to be the great provider, but we can't honestly claim any personality traits that endear us to them. It's the hand that feeds them that they like rather than the psyche of the feeder.

But back to Mr. and Mrs. Noah. I can't believe that the loading of the Ark proceeded without a hitch. Those pictures of the animals, two by two, marching meekly up the ramp into the Barnboat are a figment of the imagination of a latter-day public relations man. Our animals *never* go gently into that or any other dark nest. Pigs balk, scream, and put their considerable weight into resisting going up a ramp into our counterpart of the Ark—a pickup truck. The geese have instant nervous breakdowns, flapping and honking and falling over each other in an effort to escape impending doom even when no doom is intended. They not only announce that the sky is falling but that the earth is shaking as well.

Have you ever tried to lure two sheep out of a small enclosure? Our sheep, who always believe that the grass is greener on the other side even when they are in a lush new pasture, managed to trample down a fence that enclosed a small salad garden that was planted in their pasture long before it was a pasture. The garden is very small, probably only eight by ten feet. When we found them in there happily finishing off the lettuce, dill, and endive, the fence looked intact, but we could see that they had bent it down and leaped

over it. Do you think they would leap back out? Of course not! George had me hold up one side of the fence, and he got inside intending to shoo them out. But they galloped round and round the periphery like circus horses, completely ignoring the wide exit I was so kindly providing for them. George galloped at their heels, commenting loudly on their low I.Q.'s and punctuating his derogatory remarks with smart blows on their rumps. The two geese, who would follow the sheep into the jaws of Hades, were also in the parade, flapping and squawking. George finally had to catch each goose and throw it over the fence. Did they spread their wings and come in for a graceful landing? They did not! They crashed *Boink!* on their keels with an "Oof" as the breath was knocked out of them. Then he grabbed the sheep one at a time and shoved them through the opening. Never overestimate the common sense of either breed.

When we acquired our sheep as teenage lambs from Julie and Bob Northrup, we had planned to put them in the back of the truck for the ten-mile ride to our house. But the Northrups thought the lambs might jump out of the back. And if one did, of course the other would follow and probably meet with untimely fractures while the ink on the purchase check was still damp. So, at Julie's urging, we lifted them both into the cab. George drove and I sat next to him with the two sheep and my legs competing for the space under the dashboard. I had brought newspapers for the floor of the cab in case they joined us up front, but it never occurred to me to load them in so that they would face the back of the car. They tucked their snub noses under the dashboard and their woolly stubs of tails twitched merrily right in my lap. That wasn't all that was in my lap. Before we had turned out of the Northrup's driveway a shower of "raisins" rained down into my skirt. I opened the window and threw out a handful.

"What are you doing?" George shouted above the "maaas" and "baaas."

"What do you expect me to do, hoard them in my lap?"

Maybe the excitement of the ride relaxed their sphincters, but for the next nine miles I was hard pressed to keep up with the production of blessedly dry sheep manure. What if it had been a calf?

Why didn't I put the newspaper on my lap? Because eight sheep hooves had it firmly fastened to the floor. Why didn't I put the newspaper on my lap *before* we started? Well, never overestimate the common sense of the shepherdess either!

Happy the Bride
the Rain Falls On

"And the brass will crash
And the trumpets bray
And they'll cut a dash
On their wedding day."

from *The Mikado*

Vermont weddings come in all shapes and sizes, and if the traditional wedding seems to be an endangered species, it may be a timely demise. I doubt if there is a wet eye among the fathers of brides who elect to be married under the old apple tree wearing blossoms from the same tree rather than in a cathedral banked with palms. No male member of a wedding of my acquaintance approaches the ceremony with anything much cheerier than dread. But weddings should be fun. Let me tell you about one that was.

Debbie and Steve chose to be married down at the brook on the grassy bank in front of the pool and waterfall where she has spent every summer of her life. And Steve definitely preferred the gothic arches of elms to those of a church.

They chose October 9 because it was a holiday weekend,

would still be warm and dry underfoot, and presumably would be the peak of the fall foliage. It would, eh? The mercury in the thermometer slunk down into the low forties and stuck. Those clouds that are supposed to come equipped with silver linings shredded theirs up and sent them down as rain, not just a soft Irish mist, but a pelting monsoon. It not only rained the day of the wedding, it had rained the day before and the day before that. The path to the brook was running like a spring freshet. The color was there all right. In fact the scarlet and saffron of the wet leaves seemed even more luminous, but few of the guests saw them because their heads were bowed in concentration over each step in an effort to remain upright while picking their precarious way to the brook.

The normally clear waterfall was a roaring, seething, mud-colored Niagara wreathed in mist. And the pool was inching up the bank at an alarming rate. A canopy had been rented in case of a brief shower, but the weather forecast was so gloomy, it was assumed they would prefer to be married indoors. So the canopy was still just a cocoon in the garage. But the two principals arrived breathless and determined to ignore the elements and proceed as planned. So down to the brook sloshed the bridegroom, her father, and uncle and up went the canopy, flapping ominously in the gusts of wind.

Boots were borrowed from neighbors and the living room was littered with shoes as the guests tried on wool socks and alternate footgear.

Weaving through this disarray, Debbie's golden retriever Pathrushin, usually the bounciest of beasts, staggered drunkenly over shoes and boots with or without feet in them. He was the object of considerable concern. Two nights before he had been hit by a car. He had fled into the night, and though Steve and Debbie had combed the area hunting for him most of the night, he finally came back under his own power. He was not seriously hurt but the vet had suggested a tranquilizer so that he would not overexert himself racing around at the brook. One of the big anxieties had been that he would feel obliged to retrieve sticks from the pool during the wedding and present them to the guests while shaking all over them. No need to worry. He yawned, sighed audibly, and folded every few minutes, his front and rear ends marching to different drummers.

The law—in the cheerful form of Justice of the Peace Willy Cochran, a Jerichoan well versed in the ways of Vermont weather—showed up in a sou'wester and raincoat. The Muses, represented by Jim Landon and his trumpet, arrived, and he was outfitted in foul weather gear.

Umbrellas were unfurled and down sloshed the guests, picking their way through the rivulets like a procession of animated mushrooms on booted stems.

Jim had been concerned that his trumpet rendition of the wedding march might be a little overpowering so he had chosen to stand in the trees somewhat removed from the wedding party. But the roar of the waterfall gave him tough competition. This was not helped by the fact that it rained not only on his trumpet but in it as well.

Debbie's only concession to the weather was to leave her new Pappagallos in their tissue paper and wear her mother's very off-white sneakers under the long off-white wedding gown which she had made. George, the father of the bride, gallantly tried to hold an umbrella over her, but her outside sleeve was soon wet, and it was so cold that goose bumps showed through her quiana dress. The bride was not only radiant, she was laughing out loud as she struggled to keep George upright on the slippery path.

The ceremony was brief and beautiful, a quotation from

Thoreau and Debbie and Steve's own statement about marriage. Pathrushin, beribboned as best dog, sat at their feet, cocked his head, and tried to focus his eyes. The best man, ignoring the rain, leaped around snapping pictures with a dripping camera.

It was wild, wet, and wonderful, and no one fell down processing or recessing—well, no one except Steve. As he and Debbie marched back up the path, he tried to guide her over the rocky part and his slippery leather-soled shoes, relics of his Coast Guard stint, skidded out from under him. But the bride stayed upright, and only the bottom two inches of her wedding gown betrayed the vagaries of the weather.

Back at the house everyone shed wet clothes and readily accepted George's proffered drinks. The bride and groom posed for pictures. Not until they were developed was it noticed that Steve was in his shirtsleeves, having removed his muddy jacket, and that peeking out from under Debbie's muddy hem were the canvas toes of her mother's sneakers. There was also a recumbent shoe in the foreground.

They cut the first slice of their flower-decked, three-tiered wedding cake with an enormous Costa Rican machete adorned with scarlet leather streamers. Debbie's sister and her husband phoned from Finland. Old friends phoned from Wyoming. Absent relatives and present ones were toasted in champagne, and the bride and groom took off in a shower of rice and, you guessed it, rain!

Pumpkins

I don't know anything that gives a bigger return on your initial investment than a fifty-cent packet of pumpkin seeds. A little flat package contains perhaps two dozen seeds weighing only a fraction of an ounce. Tuck them in the ground and you have a quarter of an acre or a whole backyard full of pumpkin vines that can be counted on to produce a half-ton of pumpkins, not only in your backyard but probably in your neighbor's, whether he shares your enthusiasm for pumpkins or not. Of course there are only a few people in the world who want a backyard full of pumpkins and I'm not one of them.

It is apparently impossible for me to plant part of a packet of seeds. If a pinch of lettuce or parsley seed is good, the whole package must be better. And who has the self-control to plant one hill of summer squash or pumpkins? A sensible gardener, that's who. We frequently have had a hedge of parsley, rows of bolting lettuce, and pumpkin tendrils strangling the beets, shading the green beans into anemia, and trailing off into the meadow fifty feet from where the innocuous-looking seed was planted.

When we no longer lived on a farm in Vermont and had to adjust our rural habits to suburban Boston, we excluded pumpkins from our small vegetable garden. That shouldn't have been much of a hardship. Our girls haven't gone out trick or treating in years and theoretically they have outgrown carving jack-o-lanterns. Ours isn't a very theoretical family, however, because both of them admitted they bought little pumpkins to have at college. Bought a pumpkin? Why, I remember when I hauled thirty golden globes down to Mark Bolton's I.G.A. store in South Burlington after we had given away the biggest and best to every child in the neighborhood. There is no such thing as having the right number of pumpkins. You either have a truckload or none.

It all started the first summer in Jericho when we still spent the winters in New York City. I bought our seeds in Bloomingdale's, thinking that it might be nice to have a few pumpkins for pie. The packet was marked *Connecticut Field*. That was my first mistake. The picture on the packet showed a nice, round, absolutely perfect, orange pumpkin with nothing to show its size in relation to anything else. By mid-July our pumpkins were the size of softballs. By mid-August they were basketball size, and by the end of August, Wayne Nealy, from whom we had bought the farm, suggested that I take them to the fair.

Ridiculous! This was the first garden we had ever planted and I hadn't known enough to plant pie pumpkins. But even if I was being teased for being a city slicker, the best way to turn the joke was to call his bluff.

George was in New York, so the small girls and I huffed and puffed and lugged the three biggest pumpkins up from the garden. That is, I lugged and they huffed and puffed sympathetically because they couldn't lift one of the big pumpkins off the ground. They weighed nearly forty pounds apiece, and you can't carry a pumpkin that big by its stem, unless you like having your fingers perforated by the prickles or watching the stem snap off and the pumpkin crash to the ground and split. You just hug its slippery sides and stumble along unable to see over the top.

We washed our three specimens and set them on the floor of the car. There was no time to wash the children, so I set them on the seat of the car and we took off for Essex Junction and the Champlain Valley Fairgrounds. As exhibitors we were given a free pass and drove through the gate to the fruit and vegetable building. The clock struck twelve and our pumpkins seemed to be changing, not into golden coaches but into much smaller, much greener, and much more lopsided insignificant globes. I wanted to forget the whole thing and retreat, but how do you explain that to wide-eyed, pigtailed little girls? So I entered our ugly old cucurbits, received the number 1356, and was told they would be judged the next day. Two days later I peeked in the newspaper for the announcement of prizes, but the vegetable awards were not published. There was a beautiful picture of the largest pumpkin which didn't look familiar at all. Now I had to know. I heaved the children into the car again, heaved the kittens out again, and went heigh-ho off to the fair again, this time to pay our admission and stroll casually through the exhibits. Casually, that is, until I sidled into the fruit and vegetable building. I could see a blue ribbon attached to three enormous beauties just inside the door. But who had won the second and third places? Swallowing my pride, I asked the girl at the desk what numbers had won the other pumpkin awards.

"The children want to know, heh—heh."

The children looked surprised and I grinned foolishly.

"The second award for field pumpkins. Let's see. That's

number 1356."

"1356! That's us! We won an award." Fifty cents in cash and a foot inside the Pearly Gates.

"Burlington, Vermont, calling New York City. Eighty-five cents for the first three minutes, please."

"George? What do you think happened? No, the kids are fine. No, there nothing wrong with your plumbing. George, *listen* to me! The most marvelous thing happened. Our pumpkins won second place at the Champlain Valley Fair!"

Reflections in an
Autumn Pool

When do you turn the corner from summer into fall? Is it on the day after Labor Day when the yellow school buses lumber up into the hills to gather up the chattering children, nervous and clumsy in their bright new outsized and un-scuffed shoes?

Although school children have always tried to ignore the early signs of fall with the same dedication with which they seek out the least intimation of spring, autumn really begins on a night in August when there is an unaccustomed chill in the air, the stars are especially bright, and the last meteor of the season comes unstrung and streaks across the sky. The calendar still calls it summer when the tops of the potatoes show brown and the kernels of the sweetcorn squirt with less vigor under the sharp pressure of your fingernail. The color of the sky deepens at the zenith to gentian blue. Sky color in Vermont seems to match the predominant blue flower of the season. The spring sky is skimmed-milk blue like bluets. Summer sky blue is repeated along the edges of every road in the chicory blossoms, and the blue of late September's sky is reflected and intensified in the closed gentians that fringe our brook.

There is a gradual crescendo of color tones as first the swamp maples turn crimson and a bright splash or two of flame lights up one side of the sugar maples. Tomatoes that had threatened to live out their lives as evergreens now parade across every farm kitchen windowsill in scarlet array. Green pumpkins that have wandered out into the tall grass at the edge of the garden show golden undersides when turned over. The grass mercifully slows down its rate of metabolism, and the whine of power mowers is heard no more in the land. Kitchens are astringent with vinegar, cloves, and mustard seed or dill simmering in wait for bowls of salted sliced cucumbers, peppers, and onions that are giving up their excess juices.

Fall is a treasure hunt, discovering one more pumpkin hidden in the grass and the last nubbins of corn which are starchy but cherished because they are the last. It is exciting to ease a digging fork under each potato plant and turn up an unknown number of smooth, thin-skinned beauties and a handful of miniature new potatoes, firm and flavorful when boiled in their skins and tossed in butter and chopped parsley. After the conflagration of October has subsided, we discover the final treasure, nature's last green which, like her first, is gold; the varied ochres of wild grasses and corn stalks, bright plumes of asparagus, and a handful of elm leaves floating on a frost-rimmed pool—the only gold of the year that lasts.

I'm Tired of Keeping a Stiff Upper Lib!

The Women's Liberation Movement can just keep moving as far as I'm concerned. I've got all the rights and freedoms I can handle and a few I'm thinking of turning in to the men's lost-and-found department.

My unliberated mother never was drafted as the second man on the other end of a two-man saw. She was denied the right to change a tire, chase a pig, bury a dead raccoon, and paper the living room. She never knew she was exploited because she did not work nine-to-five in an office and then five-to-nine at home.

I don't feel demeaned when a young man helps me carry an ailing television set into a repair shop, and I get positively euphoric when a man of any age holds a door for me instead of letting it slam in my face.

I taught school for seven years and though I switched from caring for other people's children for profit to caring for our own for fun—or so I remember it through the pink haze of time—I still feel pampered and indulged because I don't have to rush to the subway at the exact time each morning. It might come as a shock to Betty Friedan to learn that the great thing about being self-employed at home is the freedom to shuffle the jobs, the leisure moments, and the spontaneous excursions to suit yourself. No school or office job can offer this.

Now I'm not saying it's all smooth sailing on the home front. I distinctly remember wishing that our first baby could extend her stay at the hospital where people knew one end of a baby from the other, while I went home for a week or so. Night feedings, picking up 1001 unmatched socks, toys, small bits of puzzles, and adhesive strands of cold spaghetti are diversions I have happily put behind me; but from the day when our youngest clambered up the high steps of the yellow school bus to the present, I feel I have been more than adequately recompensed for the work I've done. In fact, I could not have earned enough to keep myself clothed, fed, and motorized in the manner to which my husband has accustomed me. Not because I was paid less for my job than a man would have been but because doctors earn more money than nursery school teachers.

So look who's been liberated and by whom, none other than the chap I'm supposed to regard as a male chauvinist pig. Which, by the way, isn't a very insulting epithet after all. As a matter of fact, having raised pigs, we have a lot of respect and fondness for them. Certainly he enjoys being called male and the word *chauvinism* came from Chauvin whose fault was his exaggerated patriotism to Napoleon! Now you are going to say that in current usage male chauvinism means exaggerated patriotism to maleness and hence the concept of male superiority. I maintain that *any* conviction of superiority is obnoxious. Is militant feminism any less so?

All I'm saying is that the sort of freedom everyone needs is simply freedom of choice. I not only feel liberated because my husband supports me so that I can be a free-lance writer, I think the liberator deserves better than name-calling.

There are times when *out* looks good to any wife and mother, but the totally free life with no attachments can be lonely enough to make *in* look pretty good, too. So I'm asking for equal time on that perch that used to be a pedestal, but now looks more like a soap box, to say a good word for the M.C.P. who makes out the income taxes, checks the water in the car batteries, insures his life making me the beneficiary, cleans the chicken coop, loads the dishwasher, repairs the coffee grinder, and does not treat me like one of the boys. He treats me like a woman which, according to the *Oxford Dictionary*, is "an adult female human being."

What's so bad about that? I enjoy being a woman, but I'm not militant about it. The life of an Amazon is full of slings and arrows. And in spite of my fondness for pigs, who wants to be a female chauvinist sow? I've got a legalized, live-in liberator. Gloria, Germaine, and Betty, eat your hearts out!

What's Good about November?

Last March, Faith Dunne's article "In Defense of Mud Season" concluded with the question, "Does anyone want to defend the end of November?"

There is a contrary streak in most Vermonters that rises to any challenge. Yankee orneriness compels us to pick up the gauntlet, or more exactly, the soggy mitten.

True, the extravaganza of October is over and the colors in the tapestry of leaves on the ground are fading, but forgotten mini-vistas concealed during the foliage months suddenly reappear like old friends and the plume of smoke from a distant farmhouse is a reassurance of neighbors.

Oddly enough nature's last green, as Robert Frost assured us of its first, is gold. Tamaracks smolder like torches among the evergreens, piles of pumpkins overflow the periphery of roadside stands, and the gold of September goldenrod is bequeathed to asparagus tops and milkweed pods. On the dark surface of our pond a handful of golden birch leaves circles leisurely at the foot of the waterfall.

Cape Cod, with its gentle climate, holds the garnet of its oak leaves and the crimson of the cranberry bogs long after the conflagration of the hardwoods on the mainland has subsided.

But in no part of our country as much as in New England is Thanksgiving such a celebration of homecoming and family reunion as well as feasting and football. And perhaps fragrance, as Henry Beston said, "touching the emotion directly, not only wakes in us an emotion of place, but summons up as well a poignant emotion of ourselves as we were in times and the place remembered."

We were aware of this when we found a letter describing Thanksgiving as it was celebrated in our old farmhouse. Although written more than a century ago, the letter recalled a much earlier Thanksgiving. The year was 1808. "All the absent children were expected to be there and we all lotted much on being a reunited family, and I remember mother for some years had two or three poor people that she invited so as to make the day a happy one for them. Every year we used to make cider applesauce a week or two before Thanksgiving, a half barrel of it to freeze for the winter. Those were very busy days; so many kinds of pies and puddings.

"I remember when mother used to make a dozen or fifteen mince pies and freeze them, but later she made a large quantity of mince meat and froze it, then thawed it out as she wanted it. How we children used to like to go to the pantry and count the different kinds of pies, mince, apple and pumpkin, three kinds of puddings, one large baked Indian pudding in a six-quart pan, a rice pudding in a four-quart dish, and a cracker pudding for the center of the table. The large puddings were placed at the ends of the table and plenty of pies scattered all around. We raised geese, so always had a goose roasted in a baker before the fireplace. It could be easily turned."

I'm sure it could be a small boy who hoped that the turning

would hasten the magic moment when it would be done. Nearly two hundred years have not altered the images of a country kitchen evoked by those same fragrances. One of the great satisfactions of living in the country is the sense of self-reliance generated by growing and harvesting much of our own food. The aroma of a roasting turkey which you have raised yourself, redolent of your own sage and onions and sausage meat from your own pigs, the spicy fragrance oozing out of pies made from your own apples and pumpkins, the scent of the dark, moist earth as you pry up a few carrots, ice cold and brittle-crisp, and snatch a handful of parsley, still green under its insulating blanket of rotting leaves—these all evoke memories of other Thanksgivings stretching back to the first feast celebrated in Massachusetts.

There is no more comforting contrast than to stamp in out of a snow-dusted November afternoon into the fragrant warmth of a country kitchen. A glowing hearth, aromas of good food cooking, and the laughter of family and friends are elemental satisfactions.

November may not have the ephemeral charm of spring or the exuberance of summer but a country house sighs and settles on a late November night, sheltering the bounty of the harvest season, jars of jellies and pickles on the shelves, rows of pumpkins and squash lined up beneath string bags of onions and enough potatoes to last through until spring.

Let the snow come! It is this awareness of having worked in tandem with nature that nurtures the countryman's spirit.

Our Country Night Life

After our city friends get through asking what we *do* all winter in the country and are temporarily diverted by our protests that we do all the things they do but in a more copacetic environment, there is a moment of silence before the inevitable next question.

"But don't you miss the night life?"

Now what they mean by night life is the theater and concerts, most of which we have half an hour away. As a matter of fact it takes them longer than that to take a taxi to Broadway and 44th Street from the east 70s. But it is more fun to say, "No, *you* miss the night life we watch from the warm side of our living room window."

The only place you can see a snowshoe hare in New York City is the Museum of Natural History, and he is on the immobile side of the glass. Nor is an evening walk through Central Park rewarded by a glimpse of a barred owl or the undulating streak of an ermine. Not that Central Park is lacking in predators, but I prefer the wild ones who are trying to keep nature in balance to the unbalanced two-legged variety.

We do have masked bandits. When we turn the porch light

on there may be a raccoon trying to dislodge the suet from its wire basket. But we stare at each other with mutual curiosity rather than fear. We support either a couple of hyperactive snowshoe hares or a herd of less athletic ones because our woods and lawn are closely stencilled with their ornamental tracks. Deer, porcupines, skunks, and an assortment of deer mice, voles, shrews, and a woodland jumping mouse who thinks he is a kangaroo perform a continuous drama in their roles of hunter and hunted.

A new one to us this winter was the ermine. One morning we found one laying hen dead in the chicken house. Her head was missing, but there was no blood and the body was untouched. It had to be a weasel because there were no access holes big enough for a raccoon or even a fox, and each of those would have been interested in a chicken dinner either at our place in the case of a raccoon or at his if it were a fox.

We set out the Havahart trap and two old spring traps that we disapprove of in the grain room next to the hens' quarters. The next morning there was another dead chicken in the middle of the floor with only a small mark on her neck. But the door between the chicken coop and the grain room was open, the hens were all over the place, and each spring trap held a protesting chicken by the leg. The weasel must have thrashed around with his prey knocking the door open, and the other hens with their usual hysterical response rushed out in all directions, stepping witlessly right into the two traps. The flaps on the Havahart were down, but it was unoccupied. By practically dislocating my thumb I was able to release the two captives unharmed, but the two humans involved were developing an acute case of paranoia.

We baited the Havahart with a scrap of raw beef and the next morning guess who peered out from its cage? A slender snow white ermine with a black tip on his long tail. We studied each other nervously, I with admiration for his royal robe and he with understandable loathing for the human scent. It seemed impossible that this delicate creature—his body was no longer than eight inches and his tail was another six—would have attacked a five-pound fowl. It would be comparable to a human biting the neck of an elephant for which I have never had either the teeth or the least inclination.

A few nights later I turned on the porch light and was startled to see what I thought at first was a red squirrel sail from the bird feeder to a nearby pine tree. But the face that shyly peeked around a branch at me was not that of a red squirrel. The ears were larger, and the eyes had a quizzical look as though he had raised eyebrows. Besides, our red squirrels are not nocturnal. When he leapt again I could see that he had thick ridges of dark fur stretched between his forelegs and hind legs on each side. It was a flying squirrel, that shy, nervous aerialist that I had previously seen only in wildlife illustrations.

Our night life is mercifully free from electrically amplified sound and wins easily over its metropolitan counterpart in wildness and melodrama. But its special excellence is the atavistic response it evokes that quickens the pulse when the drama of life and death, courage and violence is played live and unrehearsed an arm's length away.

Cops and Robbers

I grew up in that gentle era when "Cops and Robbers" was a game for children. Although my adult experiences with cops and robbers hardly come under the heading of fun and games, there have been comic moments which seem more so in the tense atmosphere of anger and loss.

I have no friends or relations in either guild, but I have had close if involuntary contact with both. We have been robbed nine times which is just about nine times too often. You may wonder why we didn't move. We did, but not for that reason. The nine robberies were in six different apartments or houses in four different states: twice in New York City, once in Ardsley, New York; once in Weston, Massachusetts; four times in Vermont; and once in Kansas City. But in fairness to Vermont where we lived year round for nine pilferless years in South Burlington, three of our Vermont robberies were break-ins at our summer house in Jericho when it was closed for the winter.

What did we have that attracted larceny? Very little. As a matter of fact we have been a big disappointment to each of our thieves. Three times we were not only right in the house, we opened the door and unwittingly invited our robber in! The only houses in which we were never robbed were the two that were never locked. Don't try these facts on your computer. The only thing that happened every single time was some light touch of comic relief. It wasn't much relief, but it was invariably comic.

The first robbery was in our first tiny one-and-a-half-room apartment across the street from New York Hospital. We were away for the weekend and our Sunday *New York Times* on the doormat advertised that fact. Our burglar stuffed the keyhole with matchsticks which would slow us down in opening the door long enough for him to leave by way of the fire escape if we came home while he was there. When we pried out the keyhole and opened the door, he was gone but so were some of our few valuables. The dresser drawers were open, and the closets had been ransacked; and he had taken a movie projector, George's Phi Beta Kappa key, and my college class ring. Our only possession of considerable value, a chest of solid silver, was in full view and untouched. But on the coffee table there was a bowl of lichi nuts and our robber was curious enough to crack several open, nibble at them, and spit them out on the floor.

Some years later we moved down the street to a new apartment building at the corner of York Avenue and 63rd Street. It was just being finished and workmen were in and out of the apartments, installing the light fixtures and waxing the floors. So when a large, white-haired, grandfatherly looking gentleman in blue overalls and jacket rang the bell and said he was a steam fitter, I let him in without a shadow of a doubt about his credentials. He was fussing around with a radiator, so I went into the kitchen and washed the breakfast dishes. A few minutes after he left I went to pick up my pocketbook in the bedroom and it was gone. I called the super, and while he admitted there were no steam fitters working in the building, he insisted that I had mislaid my pocketbook. I hunted everywhere. No luck and besides I knew it had been on the bed. I reported it again to the super who regarded me with a bored expression. I phoned the police who took a description of the man and my name and address only to shut me up.

A week later the doorbell rang again and there stood my elderly and apparently not too bright steam fitter! With pounding heart I told him to come back in a few minutes and then I called the super on the house phone and begged him frantically to come up. He did, with the doorman, and they surprised the old gent next door with two other pocketbooks tucked under his jacket. He was escorted down to the lobby. A police car sirened up, and the police took him away. Later that afternoon the phone rang.

"Mrs. Wolf? This is Detective Ryan at the precinct station. I'm happy to tell you that we have caught your man."

"*You've* caught him?" I squawked. "I caught him and I had to rub your nose in his tracks to do it."

The next day he phoned again to ask if I would appear in court to identify our robber. It was a long subway ride and a longer wait. All I was allowed to contribute was "yes" when they asked if that was the man whose disappearance coincided with that of my purse. It turned out that this sweet-faced old boy had spent thirty of his seventy years in prison for this type of offense. But my policeman who by now had adopted me as the precinct mascot said he would take me home.

"You can ride on my badge," he offered magnanimously, and while I hardly thought that looked comfortable, I was all for the idea of free transportation with my own police escort. But we didn't travel in a police car or even on a motorcyle. We rode uptown on the Lexington Avenue subway. He muttered something to the lady in the change booth at the subway station, and we walked through a side gate without paying. As I sailed ahead my guardian Irishman grabbed my wrist and winked broadly.

"Listen, you can't sashay ahead like that. Stick close to me. Don't you know you are supposed to be handcuffed to me? You are riding as my prisoner!"

Within a year after we bought a little house in Ardsley, George was asked to be Dean at the University of Vermont College of Medicine and we put our house on the market by running an ad in the Sunday *New York Times*. Hordes of people stamped through the house all day Sunday. On Monday a man phoned to ask if he could see the house and if I could meet him at the train. We were so eager to make a sale without an agent that I met him, drove him home, and showed him the house. He then asked if he could use the bathroom. I even set out a fresh towel for him! Much later I discovered that my engagement ring, which had been on the shelf of the medicine cabinet, was missing. I couldn't believe it, but it never turned up.

In the years when we lived in South Burlington, Vermont, we never locked the house in the winter. In fact we had to hunt around for the antique key to the front door when we went on a trip. But the little summer house we have had in Jericho for thirty years has been broken into several times. We don't resent the occasional hunter who comes in for shelter. He never takes anything, and we only know of these visits because one of our blankets will be left in a chair where he has wrapped himself up. But we were not happy about the uninvited guest who smashed a window to get in, smeared mustard on the floor, left beer cans scattered about, and helped himself to an old toaster. We knew there was nothing of value in the Jericho house. Our vandals apparently agreed, but those old appliances were useful to us in the summer.

Our first house in Weston, Massachusetts, was unlocked and unmolested. We had no dog but everyone around us had one, two, or even three. This didn't fascinate me especially but may have been a deterrent to prowlers. Our second house in Weston was never entered by force. Once again I unwittingly ushered in a light-fingered visitor. We had to sell the house when we moved to Kansas. The real estate agent always came with prospective buyers and took them around from room to room. Hardly a setting for the perfect crime but one day she came with three ladies. One must have lagged behind sufficiently to remove my pocketbook from the desk in the kitchen. Served her right too! There was nothing in it. I had just transferred my money, car keys, and credit cards to another bag because I was going into Boston. It was almost worth it to imagine her expression when she got rid of the agent and opened the bag!

Our most recent robbery was last fall. Only an hour elapsed between the time when I left the house and the time when George came home. Our new little house is always kept locked. So is the garage. We have a crime alert sticker in the window. George has engraved his social security number on every possible appliance in the house, and we have automatic lights which go on at dusk. But these chaps went around to the wooded back side of the house and pried out a heavy, double-paned, locked Anderson window. They didn't break the glass but they didn't do the wood around the frame any good.

Every drawer and closet was ransacked. My jewelry was spread out on the bed and the few valuable pieces were taken—my mother's engagement diamond, my sister's circle of diamonds, and my own twenty-fifth wedding anniversary pearl ring. They also took a radio, two guns, a Swiss army knife, and a roll of stamps. They apparently wrapped the guns in a big felt Snoopy banner, a present to George when he got his pilot's license.

A few weeks later when these same robbers set fire to a building in Winooski to divert attention from a robbery they had planned at a nearby Grand Union, they were caught. How did the police know they were responsible for our robbery? Because when their apartment was searched there was Snoopy with his words, "Curse you Red Baron" hanging at the window.

But our worst robbery in terms of loss was done in grand style in Kansas City. We lived in an enormous beautiful Tudor mansion that went with the job. You would think that it contained art treasures, furs, and jewels. That's what you'd think unless you knew us. We didn't own a diamond at that time. Remember that my engagement ring left us in Ardsley. Nor did we have dead minks or Manets. This house was kept carefully locked which was no minor flip of the latch-string. There were five outside doors on the first floor and two in the basement. But I patrolled them like a police dog, and it would have been better if I had let a police dog do it. One morning I went out at ten, returned an hour later, and came in through the garage. As I came upstairs and into the butler's pantry I saw that all the drawers were pulled out. Two chests of solid silver, ours and George's mother's, were gone. In fact, every piece of silver except three knives in the dishwasher were gone. All the first floor outside doors were hanging wide open for easy egress and every closet upstairs and down had been searched. An old safe deposit box had been thrown on the floor when the robber discovered that it contained Patty's diaries instead of cash. The only loot taken from George's bureau included several Kennedy half dollars, a steel-cased Cartier watch, and George's father's gold cuff links. There were many finger marks but all bore the imprint of cotton gloves. His taste was excellent. He took one look at my thirty-year-old muskrat coat and discarded it on the hall floor. I could almost hear him saying, "Yuk!"

The police came after two phone calls. I first called the nearest police station only to have it explained to me in great detail that our house was just over the line and came under the jurisdiction of the Prairie Village Police Department instead of the Fairway Police Department. If our robber had still been in the house, this would have given him a good head start. I wasn't sure that he was not, so I had phoned from next door and waited outside for the police. The young officer searched the house from attic to cellar with me trotting nervously at his heels. He admonished me not to touch anything including a man's hat on the floor which I knew belonged to George.

Finally he sat down, pulled out his papers, pushed up his sleeves, licked his pencil, and cleared his throat.

"Now ma'am if you'll just answer a few routine questions. Let's see now, how do you 'spose you spell "entered," with an i or an e?"

Oh well, I was overdue for the comic relief, and no one ever promised that the long arm of the law could reach as far as the spelling book.

The Winter of My Content

No one had prepared us for the little pleasures of living in the woods in winter. We were awash in dire predictions of deep snow, icy roads, power failures, and frozen pipes. Even more gloomy was the predictable reaction when we said we planned to become "year-round summer folk."

"Oh, I know Vermont is beautiful, but I'd hate the long winter. And won't you feel dreadfully isolated?"

City people, or even suburban folk, and we have been both, think of winter in terms of snow plowing and icy roads. So do we, but they are *less* of a problem in the country. City streets are so clogged with parked cars and traffic that they are cleared very slowly and inadequately. Residential suburban streets are the last to be plowed because the town equipment is busy on the thoroughfares. We live one mile from the hard-topped road and that mile of gravel road—oh, all right—dirt road, is plowed right along with the hard top because the big tank truck that bears the incongruous sign "Moo Juice Express" has to get our neighbors' milk out at the same time every day. We have fewer days when the roads are icy than we did when we lived in Westchester, Boston, or

Kansas City because freezing rain is unusual here. When it gets cold, it stays that way—none of this shilly-shallying around just above and below thirty-two degrees.

The real anxieties, and I admit there are some in winter, are the possibility of a power failure and the possibility of freezing pipes. We worry about those because if our power was off for any length of time we would have no central heat, no running water, no electric light, no electric stove, and no refrigerator. Now that's not as bad as it sounds. The fireplace would do for a short time. Water could be hauled from the spring. All women love candlelight. A refrigerator is redundant in the middle of winter, and we could cook quite a lot in the fireplace and over the charcoal grill. But without the pump to keep the water moving in the pipes, they would freeze solid if it were very cold. That's a possibility that motivated us to install a generator but far less likely than being robbed in Manhattan or other cities. We were robbed in New York, Kansas City, and Westchester. The longest power failure we have ever experienced was not in Vermont but in Kansas City. When it is near zero we let the water run in the bathroom just to keep it moving in the pipes. Fortunately our new well runneth over so we can afford to be a bit prodigal with water.

There is another misfortune that is supposed to befall us—isolation.

"You'll be so cut off from everything."

Being snowed in is a wonderful cozy feeling, only it just doesn't happen. Once years ago when we lived in the country in South Burlington, we were snowed in for a day. George couldn't get to his office, and the children couldn't get to school. I didn't hear much wailing or gnashing of teeth. It was a real holiday, and the girls complained bitterly when our driveway was plowed and school reopened the next day. It is even less likely now because we have a snow blower. That wouldn't keep the schools open, but our children are long past school age. It takes George about ten minutes to blow out the driveway and become mobile again. So being snowed in is a luxury we will probably have to forego.

And what is this specter of isolation? What is the "everything" that is going to be out of our reach? Traffic, theater, concerts, restaurants, some parties, shopping?

Obviously we don't miss the traffic jams. Honestly we don't miss the theater, concerts, and restaurants because they were only a myth in our life in New York anyway. Most New Yorkers think that proximity to culture automatically makes them cultured. When we lived in the city, we rarely went to a play or concert. When we had the inclination in the first few years, we didn't have the money. When we had the money, the inclination disappeared because it was constantly available. The concerts and lectures at the University here are twenty-five minutes away. When we lived on East 63rd Street, it took us that long to get across town and down twenty blocks. Now it would take twice as long and cost two dollars in a taxi each way. We have a record player and a television, and our greatest luxury is reading. Although I love the party atmosphere of eating out, George would be perfectly happy to eat at home every night, and I would, too, at least most of the time. About once a month he has a meeting in Washington, New York, or Boston, and about every other month I go with him and try a new restaurant or an old favorite. Each time I come back convinced that we were very smart to move to the country. Cocktail parties? Have you ever been to one that you preferred to a small dinner with a few friends? I always think I will miss the big stores, but when I am in the city and wander through them, I rarely buy anything because the same things are here in Burlington.

Well, maybe not Charles Jourdan shoes or Gucci bags, but they would feel out of place in my closet anyway.

But what nobody tells you is that winter in the country is a window of wildness, a time of seeing things as they really are and of being a part of the drama of wild life that comes right up to our door. There is no other season when you can tell just what has happened during the night. A deer mouse came out of the woods, crossed the deck, had a brief scuffle, and dashed under the porch. A red squirrel jumped from the nearest pine tree, gleaned the seeds the chicadees had twitched off the feeder, and ran back up the next pine tree. A deer came up our path from the brook, pawed at the straw covering our pipe line, and moved on to the tastier hay banked around the house. Something startled him because he bounded away into an alder thicket in great leaps. George got up in the night for a drink of water and looked out the kitchen window into the upturned wide eyes and sooty twitching nose of a snowshoe rabbit sitting on our deck two feet away from him. I've never seen him, but almost every night his big fluffy hind footprints go all the way around the house and then back into the woods. In the summer we see more cottontails than we care to, but I wouldn't have known we had snowshoe hares if the nightly edition of the footprint news didn't keep me *au courant*.

It frequently snows during the night, preparing an unmarked page for the news about our human neighbors as well. Footsteps have come out of the Cross's house, big ones and medium-sized ones. That means both Jack and Joan have gone out this morning. I can tell if the mailman has come by his tire tracks curving in towards the mailbox. June Manor has been home for the weekend because there are Volkswagen tracks at the side of the house. A large man's footprints come part way up to our house and then go back

118

to the road.

But while all this activity is informative, it is the silence of winter that restores my soul. Thoreau said, "This stillness, solitude, wildness of nature is a kind of thoroughwort or boneset to my intellect."

When I walk down the path to the brook, I hear only an occasional soft "pluff" as a pine bough unloads its burden of snow and bounds upward. The gurgle of the waterfall is muffled because it now flows under a cascade of icefalls. The shape of the pool is constantly changing, sometimes almost all snow-covered with just an onyx eye of open water under the waterfall. There are tracks of small animals on the snow-covered ice where they have come to drink at the edge of the Stygian pool. Sometimes the pines are laden with six inches of snow and the slender white birches arc into hoops like girls with their heads bent down combing their long hair towards their bare toes. The rocks look like crouching polar bears and each fence post wears a fat marshmallow on top. A house or barn that I had never noticed before emerges now that the leaves have fallen.

The distinctive wine glass shape of an elm, the widespread craggy arms of an oak, or the gnarled cupped hands of an apple tree label the species more clearly at a distance than if they were in leaf. And I have been surprised this winter at the amount of color in what we think of as the muted season. The osiers are crimson, and there is a frosted purple bloom on the black raspberry canes. The various browns of the weeds and ferns poking up out of the snow have the mellow warmth of wood tones—chestnut, mahogany, and pale ash. Weeping willows glow golden even in winter, and the apple twigs, last year's growth, have a rosy sheen. Winter sunsets are citrus colored—tangerine, pale lime, and lemon yellow. The same golden and pale wash of green are reflected on the breasts of the evening grosbeaks splitting open the sunflower seeds on our feeder. Tiny rainbows flash and sparkle everywhere on the surface of the new snow, and in the distance the snow-covered mountains turn from pale mauve to rosy purple in the late afternoon. After a big storm the meadows are seas of white, drifted and swirled into waves that crest and throw off a spume of fine snow dust like spray.

We enjoy people and need them, but even more we need and enjoy this lovely feeling of being insulated against smog, black city dirt, and the jackhammers of noise and crowds. It was more than three hundred years ago when John Donne wrote "No man is an island, entire of itself." While that is still true, it has become even more true that every man yearns for an island, a place where he can be surrounded by whatever nourishes his individual spirit. Perhaps some people can build their islands within the city and get their nourishment—or is it only frenetic energy—from the constant stimulation of all of their senses. I, too, once found Manhattan wonderfully exciting. But that was thirty years ago when we could stroll in Central Park on summer evenings, ride on the top of a Fifth Avenue bus, or find a parking place within a block of our destination. Now I prefer the natural colors of a sunset to neon lights, the chuckling of our brook to the assault of pneumatic drills, the taste of apple pie to French pastry, the smell of arbutus to exhaust fumes, and space around me instead of bodies in the subway. I like islands, frames of quiet or distance to set off the notes of a hermit thrush or the beauty of a snow-capped mountain.

It is all very simple and goes back to Antaeus, who was, as we all once were, a child of the sea. He became stronger when he touched the earth. And so do I.

The Uncommon Christmas

It began to look a lot like Christmas even before Halloween this year, but what seemed like a personal affront in October now is just the frosting on the holiday cake. Christmas is supposed to be snowy in northern Vermont and usually is. No palm trees or pink plastic pines for us! I don't even like green plastic pines or natural trees that have been sprayed with very unnatural green.

Now that Christmas is upon us and we are either ankle-deep in wrappings and bits of Scotch tape that stick to the wrapper instead of the wrappee, or elbow-deep in flour and cookie dough, what is it that makes one Christmas stand out from all the others, a recurrent memory that is as lustrous as a Christmas tree ornament?

Is it the remembrance of a childhood Christmas when you awoke before dawn and realized that this was *it* and that downstairs, hanging from the mantel was your stocking, knobby with unknown treasure?

Or was it the first Christmas in your own apartment when your Christmas tree may have been a parking lot reject or an evergreen branch adorned with four balls and a handful of tinsel?

What comes to mind is rarely a whole Christmas season or even a whole Christmas day but isolated moments that somehow encapsulate the essence of Christmas.

I remember our first Christmas in Vermont. We had lived in New York City for fifteen years, and though we had spent the last four summers in Vermont, this was the first time that we were "year-round summer folks." No icicle was left unturned in our efforts to reproduce a Currier and Ives country Christmas. Though we lived in the country in South Burlington with a good many wooded acres, our woods were lacking in Christmas trees so we drove out to Jericho to get our tree from the rocky hillside that was our first foothold in Vermont. Our second car at the time was a red Ford pickup truck with a cab that held the four of us illegally but cosily because Debbie was hardly big enough to cast a shadow and Patty had only a couple of inches on her in both directions.

Choosing a Christmas tree is apt to bring out the worst and best in each member of the family. Each one favors a different tree. One complains about the weather, another about the lack of intelligence of a sibling, another that she is facing imminent starvation. It usually falls to the father to point out loudly that they are on a family expedition that is supposed to be fun, and if they don't agree on a tree, they can do without. At which horrendous thought, well known as a heretic impossibility, complaints are swallowed, a choice is made, and, from that moment on, the tree, whether scraggly or lopsided, becomes the most admired one they've ever had.

In our case getting the tree involves trudging up a steep hill through the snow, tripping over concealed brambles, and getting slapped in the face with twigs that snap back from the passage of the person in front of you. It is always cold and clear, and a snowshoe hare may leap off into the woods making our hearts leap with him. After all, isn't this the way bringing home the Christmas tree is supposed to look, feel, and sound.

But that first year, cutting our own tree, cooking a turkey we had raised ourselves, and steaming a plum pudding was not enough. We had to hunt for a Yule log, too. So we all struggled across the fields into our woods, the children floundering through the snow and making snow angels every time they fell down and the dog Jet, a juvenile black labrador, bounding in great leaps through the snow. Of all the members of the family, Jet enjoyed the winter the most, rolling ecstatically in the snow, burrowing into drifts, and catching the falling flakes in his mouth.

George finally found a log which, while not quite the dimensions of King Arthur's hearth, was big enough to satisfy the children and small enough to be portable. The kids took turns carrying it, one at each end, and then George heaved it onto his shoulder hoping to make faster progress. Jet, entranced by this new game, raced in circles around George, barking enthusiastically and finally tripping him. George stumbled and the Yule log catapulted from his shoulder, its butt end catching Jet squarely on the back of the head. We all froze in horror as Jet and one third of the log disappeared into the snowdrift. The children dug furiously, pulled the log away, and uncovered a very mollified dog who staggered to his feet, shook himself experimentally, and then bounded off with a joyous bark. The blow should have at least knocked him senseless, but the deep snow had cushioned the impact and relief was rampant.

No one missed the boar's head or the wassail bowl. The warm and welcoming house was redolent of fresh evergreens and roasting turkey, onions, and mince pie. Christmas in the country was no longer an urbanite's fantasy for the future but here and now for our family to savor with all five senses—and the sixth sense of wonder, which is the spirit of Christmas.

"No Orchard's the Worse
for the Wintriest Storm"

Beyond the curve in our road there is a sugar maple that
tests my credulity each October. Its crescendo of color—from
the first flash of scarlet on one side, when the rest of the tree
is summery green, until the whole tree ignites into a torch of
red and gold—follows the same pattern each year. At close
range the luminous quality seems to come from the fact that
each yellow or apricot leaf is edged and streaked in a different
pattern of crimson. The whole tree pulses with light. Yet I
have also seen its bare branches thrashing in March winds
and its waxy new leaves crowding into a shade in May. The
tree and I are in daily communion.

The farther I have been away from our back road, in a city
or in a warmer climate, the more dependent I have been upon
this tree's affirmation of faith. It is easy to believe in evolving
life and progress when all the land is lush and green, flowering and bearing fruit, and when the sun is warm upon your
back. But Emerson wrote, "Man cannot be happy and strong
until he too lives with nature in the present." And the present
is November or February as often as it is May or July.

When the tree stands grey and dripping in the November

rains, I identify with it and feel sodden and drained of vitality. And when some of the ice-laden branches snap and crash to the ground in a February sleet storm, my courage shrinks down within me like the mercury in the thermometer.

But these are human emotions. For the tree, and all nature for that matter, winter is only a preparation for new life. Apples cannot grow without this rest period at low temperatures.

"Dread fifty above more than fifty below," Robert Frost reminds us in "Goodbye and Keep Cold." This year's leaves wither and fall, but the tree has already formed the buds for next year's foliage. They are not only there but are distinguishable as fruiting or flowering buds.

The woodchucks and raccoons don't doubt the spring as they stuff themselves so that they can live off their fat during their intermittent naps. The small, brown milkweed seeds drifting through the air on their tiny parachutes are not performing a last rite. They are on their way to the unknown spot where they will germinate in the spring.

When we are out of touch with the land—and I mean the actual feel of a handful of warm earth, the pressure of rocks under your feet—we lose the sense of balance that the immutable change of seasons brings. What reassurance is there for mankind in hi-rise boxes of concrete blocks and glass that are obsolete before they are completed, cities that are in an advanced stage of self-destruction, and industry where profit and pollution are racing for a dark victory?

But when your days and nights are defined by frost warnings and the proper tilth of the soil for planting, the awareness that there will be times of freezing rain and bitter cold is balanced by the knowledge that there will also surely be increasing warmth in the sun and unfolding of new buds.

In the dependable cycle of the seasons, blizzards and sub-zero nights—those times when the snow squeaks under your feet and nails snap like pistol shots in the walls—do not mean death; they are simply the recurrent test of faith that man needs to strengthen his affirmation of new life and growth and inevitably, even in Vermont, of spring!

About the Author

You can take the lady out of Vermont but you can't take Vermont out of the lady! Maggie Wolf is a Vermonter by choice rather than by birth, but she has one foot wedged firmly in the door by virtue of two Vermont great-grandfathers.

She was born in Montclair, New Jersey, in 1914. After graduation from Mount Holyoke College and the Bank Street College of Education, she taught at the Bank Street Nursery School and at Sarah Lawrence College. Maggie Wolf is the author of five books and regularly contributes articles to popular magazines.

The Wolfs bought their farm in Jericho in 1948 and summered there until 1952 when Dr. George Wolf was appointed dean of the University of Vermont College of Medicine and they became "year round summer folk." Nine years later they moved to Boston for five years and then to Kansas City for four years, but they always returned with their two daughters to Jericho in the summer—even if only for one month.

In 1970 they saw the handwriting on the walls of Jericho and returned to Vermont to live happily ever after. The family census has changed since 1948. Patty is now Mrs. Tage Ström and lives in Kerava, Finland, with her Finnish husband and two little boys, Patrick and Peter. Debbie is now Mrs. Stephen Page, lives in South Burlington, Vermont, and teaches at the Thayer School in Burlington.

CHRISTIAN HERALD ASSOCIATION AND ITS MINISTRIES

CHRISTIAN HERALD ASSOCIATION, founded in 1878, publishes The Christian Herald Magazine, one of the leading interdenominational religious monthlies in America. Through its wide circulation, it brings inspiring articles and the latest news of religious developments to many families. From the magazine's pages came the initiative for CHRISTIAN HERALD CHILDREN'S HOME and THE BOWERY MISSION, two individually supported not-for-profit corporations.

CHRISTIAN HERALD CHILDREN'S HOME, established in 1894, is the name for a unique and dynamic ministry to disadvantaged children, offering hope and opportunities which would not otherwise be available for reasons of poverty and neglect. The goal is to develop each child's potential and to demonstrate Christian compassion and understanding to children in need.

Mont Lawn is a permanent camp located in Bushkill, Pennsylvania. It is the focal point of a ministry which provides a healthful "vacation with a purpose" to children who without it would be confined to the streets of the city. Up to 1000 children between the ages of 7 and 11 come to Mont Lawn each year.

Christian Herald Children's Home maintains year-round contact with children by means of an *In-City Youth Ministry*. Central to its philosophy is the belief that only through sustained relationships and demonstrated concern can individual lives be truly enriched. Special emphasis is on individual guidance, spiritual and family counseling and tutoring. This follow-up ministry to inner-city children culminates for many in financial assistance toward higher education and career counseling.

THE BOWERY MISSION, located at 227 Bowery, New York City, has since 1879 been reaching out to the lost men on the Bowery, offering them what could be their last chance to rebuild their lives. Every man is fed, clothed and ministered to. Countless numbers have entered the 90-day residential rehabilitation program at the Bowery Mission. A concentrated ministry of counseling, medical care, nutrition therapy, Bible study and Gospel services awakens a man to spiritual renewal within himself.

These ministries are supported solely by the voluntary contributions of individuals and by legacies and bequests. Contributions are tax deductible. Checks should be made out either to CHRISTIAN HERALD CHILDREN'S HOME or to THE BOWERY MISSION.

**Administrative Office: 40 Overlook Drive, Chappaqua, New York 10514
Telephone: (914) 769-9000**